It occurred to me

It occurred to me

Or,

How did I get here?
An irreverent and humorous retrospective
on Public Service

Peter D Carr CBE DL

Printed in Victoria, Canada

Note for Librarians: a cataloguing record for this book that includes Dewey Classification and US Library of Congress numbers is available from the National Library of Canada. The complete cataloguing record can be obtained from the National Library's online database at:
www.nlc-bnc.ca/amicus/index-e.html
ISBN 1-4120-2083-2

TRAFFORD

This book was published on-demand in cooperation with Trafford Publishing.
On-demand publishing is a unique process and service of making a book available for retail sale to the public taking advantage of on-demand manufacturing and Internet marketing. On-demand publishing includes promotions, retail sales, manufacturing, order fulfilment, accounting and collecting royalties on behalf of the author.

Suite 6E, 2333 Government St., Victoria, B.C. V8T 4P4, CANADA
Phone 250-383-6864   Toll-free 1-888-232-4444 (Canada & US)
Fax 250-383-6804   E-mail sales@trafford.com   Web site www.trafford.com
TRAFFORD PUBLISHING IS A DIVISION OF TRAFFORD HOLDINGS LTD.

Trafford Catalogue #04-0007   www.trafford.com/robots/04-0007.html

10   9   8   7   6   5   4   3

To Geraldine
for being there

Foreword

The title of this biographical piece sets out its theme—it is about events and ideas. A few family members and colleagues, having read the draft, commented that I deal only in brief with personal relationships. Where I do so it is in the context of an event or a particular circumstance in which I found myself. Most of my close family appear only briefly in the text but this is not a measure of their influence; on the contrary the emotional impact of our relationships shaped me and set my direction.

I am not at one with those who claim in their biographies that their views and convictions have remained constant throughout life. There have been intellectual influences that have shaped my convictions and the Postscript names two of many. Nor do I claim universal correctness for my actions and beliefs. I have many regrets. In particular I fear that I carried far too much ideological baggage with me over the years. My experience in America was formative and more's the pity that the experience came later rather than earlier in life.

Whilst I might not agree with my friends and colleagues, their view and ideas have been critical in the development of my own. In particular I have to nominate Derek Robinson whose brilliant mind has illuminated so many dark recesses of my thinking on the labour market. Professor Sid Kessler, a first class teacher, has provided wise counselling over the years. The relatively short working relationship with Sir Liam Donaldson was so productive and enjoyable that its brevity has been a constant regret. George Healy, a long-standing friend, has reacted with amusement to so many of my invectives. It is within the pages of his annual gift of diaries that much of this detail has been recorded.

I owe a great debt to a former Principal of Fircroft College, Leslie Stephens, who accepted me as a student in a crucial act of faith. I have every admiration for the politically adroit Kenneth Clarke, who as a Minister, trusted me first of all with £1 million and following his move to the Health Service went on to trust me with £1.5 billion. That experience paid dividends when a subsequent Secretary of State for Health set out a radical programme of reform, in which I had the privilege to be involved.

There are so many personal friends that space could not be found to set out their contribution to my life. Of all American friends I owe a particular debt to Fred and Lisa Hoehler who phoned when our lives seemed to become a bit ragged at the edges and insisted that we cry on their sympathetic shoulders. I have valued the long friendship with Tom Donahue whom, but for quirk of fate, would have become a great President of the AFL–CIO.
Within the family I have benefited from the friendship of my brother and his good wife. Steve and Alyce, our son and daughter have my admiration and respect for their fine characters and their achievements in life; particularly against the manner in which I fumbled my way through my responsibilities as a father.

A couple of sentences in a Foreword is no way to set out the contribution to one's life of a marriage to a remarkable lady. It justifies a book beyond my capacity. Suffice here to record my eternal love and gratitude to Geraldine.

All those named above and in the text are absolved from any responsibility for the views and the ideas. I have endeavoured to avoid self-aggrandisement and there are many pages of humorous self-depreciation. Having worked with many, I am severe in my criticism of only one politician. Events are described from my distinctive perspective and I acknowledge that there will be different interpretations. I set out the part I believe I played in the harmony of events. In other word, it is my cadenza.

In its composition this labour has had our grandchildren in mind so they might know a little of their grandfather and his times. To Nelson, Warren, Elizabeth and Oscar, I dedicate this text.

PDC. 20 JANUARY 2004

One: **Silver Spoons**

It was a hot and humid October when we arrived in Washington in 1978. I had a diplomatic visa in the passport and diplomatic credentials filed with the State Department. I had a new job ahead and the stimulating prospect of studying that immense country from within. At the Embassy the in-tray spilled over with paper and on top a note, from a distinguished ex union and Labor Department official, invited my wife and I to dinner that weekend. Over the meal they asked me how I had got there. I said by plane to which they laughed. 'Now', they insisted, 'you must tell us how *you* really got *here*'. So I told them.

A DIRTY OLD TOWN

The sharpest early memories are of war: 1939 and an August holiday in Blackpool with the sultry evenings outdoors excited by the fencing searchlights limbering for a conflict to come. Then sitting with my father sometime later—perched on an athletic field wall giving welcome and other comforts to Dunkirk veterans. Or—huddled under a bed in a hospital isolation ward, fevered with diphtheria, head protected with an enamel basin, cringing at the occasional wham of an explosion and window glass splintering into the room. I recall being pretty upset too on leaving hospital to find my friends in possession of fine collections of shrapnel, which they displayed on their bedroom shelves.

My father's allotment fed us well throughout the war. He skilfully preserved new potatoes in sand—saving many for our Christmas dinner. He was good too at developing contraptions to make life easier. His device—in response to the blackout—lowered a tube over the room light when the outside door opened.

My mother's ingenuity ran to organising the steady supply of nourishing food from the butcher and the grocery stores. Even in the midst of the worst shortage she could always produce. She was skilled at managing our tiny budget and never failed to ensure the availability of funds to provide our annual holiday. For her it was an essential and treasured glimpse of other places, which she determinedly ensured we experienced all through the war years. My father, bless him, could not save; but my Mother stacked away the necessary pennies throughout the year to ensure our annual joy. She continued with considerable ingenuity, over the austerity years following the war, to find ways to accumulate the required funds. A brilliant whist player with a photographic memory, she could play a skilful hand with the sole intention of adding to the 'holiday pot'. Some years later, with a regular supply of waste materials from a local clothing factory, she produced thousands of dolls and draught excluders in the shape of daschund dogs—a very popular item in a town with open fires and badly fitting doors. A few years on she drove my father to the point of distraction when she purchased a knitting machine. It is no exaggeration to say that she virtually clothed the whole town in a range of woollen sweaters and cardigans. To any hint of criticism against her dedication she would simply retort that holidays needed to be longer and should be spent in decent hotels.

In his younger days my father was an accomplished sportsman—a soccer player with sufficient talent to be invited to join Sheffield Wednesday junior team and with the drive, co-ordination and pace to make him a valued bowler sought by all the local cricket teams. As a young man my father nurtured an ambition to achieve professional status in both games and might possibly have achieved his ambition without the ultimatum from my mother. She posed the necessary economic question. In an age when athletes were admired but unrewarded, my father was forced to choose between the glamour of sport and the harsher reality of married life. From there he contented himself with weekend sport and a more secure, but certainly duller and more routine economic existence.

PRINTING AND POLITICS

Those early war years hold other and formative memories. My father was a printer and managed the rotary machine shop of a weekly newspaper. I loved my regular visits to his workplace. Hot metal newsprint production has a smell redolent of last minute exclusive news headlines; of caustic editorial wit; of honest reporting borne of hard labour. I was always captivated by the linotype machine, which was an almost perfect conception in its original design and was hardly altered throughout its productive life. It worked with a satisfying series of mechanical clunks and on many of my visits would produce my name and address as a special treat.

The men who worked these hot metal machines were as distinct in character as the machines on which they laboured. They were literate labourers! They read more than the material they produced, they had ideas, studied books, attended libraries and talked intelligent politics over their beers.

Of all early memories, the Friday nights from this period provided inspiration and energy for many years. Friday saw the final edition of the newspaper put to bed. With luck and no mishaps in the earlier stages, the vast rotary machine would complete the production around 11 PM. My mother worked throughout the evening in sequence with the printing. By 10.30 PM with the table laid and possibly a large rabbit pie in the shiny black Yorkshire stove she would be ready to welcome my father and frequently his colleagues. With the house so perfumed by the cooking it would have been a rare torture to despatch a child to bed despite the hour. As the eldest son I often joined the adults for the meal and frequently caught the tone of the ensuing debate.

Those years, from the latter stages of the war into the depressing years of austerity, which followed, were materially mean and constricting. But down the years I carry no sense of a people beaten down by a lack of material well being. On the contrary, I have a clear memory of debate, of ideas, of propositions for political reform; of a belief in democratic politics and of the value which working people would bring to that process through their active participation. That perception is reinforced by the memory of those rabbit pie dinners and the optimism with which my parents and their friends engaged the political and economic troubles which faced them. From those dinners I recall not only optimism but also an enthusiasm for the political process which in the ensuing years has been squandered in the arrogance and incompetence of our parochial parliamentary system. Maybe my parents and their friends were, to some extent, looking for solutions to problems, which could not simply be engineered through the parliamentary system. Maybe they were all as much part of the problem as they were the agents of the solution. Ernest Bevin in a telling speech in the United States once said that 'the problem with my people is the poverty of their desire'. Whilst unchannelled avarice and greed can rip a country apart, a lack of individual aspiration can, as Bevin saw, flatten off the broader economic well being and development of the general population.

When we look around our older industrial cities and their inheritance of mean housing, in which generations continue to be born and grow—can we doubt the wisdom of Bevin's dictum? When I return to my home town and look at that depressing terrace which contains my birthplace—number 1 Briton Street—still occupied by a young family, I think of the optimism of those Friday night debates.

TOWN ROOTS

My mother's family can be traced back through the history of the town as far as written records extend. Her mother owned a bakery and provision shop, which is still remembered by a dwindling number for the quality of its brown cobs and crusty loaves. I recently talked to an old gentleman who showed me his first pair of cuff links, bought from Woolworth's seventy years before, which on purchase he had proudly rushed to show to my grandmother in her shop. He described her as the 'economic heart' of the family: hard working of course, but with the added contribution of shrewdness and skill. Harriet came to live with us in her later years but I remember her only as a frail and lonely old lady.

My grandfather's existence within our family history somewhat resembles those retouched photographs of Stalin's purged friends where those he had eliminated were painted out of existence. I could never persuade my mother, her sister Gertrude and certainly not my grandmother to talk at any length about my grandfather. I know that he had worked as a senior manager in a manufacturing company and I have heard him described by those who knew him as a 'Gaffer's Man'. He seems certainly to have been skilled in the art of language. He belonged to an expensive golf club, knew everybody in town and had an enviable skill with the ladies. For a time he worked successfully as an auctioneer, but over the years he seems to have drained my grandmother's business of any profit in order to finance his golfing and other activities. He was a close confidant of a notorious character by the name of Jack Harry White who practised as an undertaker and on occasion, just for the hell of it, my grandfather would volunteer to drive a horse drawn hearse. When I was a young man, Jack Harry told me of more than one occasion when my grandfather galloped the hearse through the town high street at break-neck speed.

Grandfather eventually flew the family nest to set up a new life with a younger woman. Maybe the failure of the bakery under his consistent plundering precipitated the departure, or maybe the attractions of the younger woman were too strong to resist. Poor man—he had little time for his new life before he suffered a stroke and lay bedridden in hospital. Yet I still award him some admiration. When my grandmother visited him in sympathy for his plight, she found that his original girlfriend had departed but that he had so charmed a visitor to the next bed, she had agreed to take him into her home. He died shortly after that but his persuasive skills, his style, and his love of life—somewhat too great for his modest income—are still remembered with affection. Who knows but that some of his more admirable traits have passed down the generations to instil themselves into the present!

MATURITY AT THIRTEEN

I left full time schooling a few days before my 14th birthday. No one could later explain how I managed that feat, but some minor illness provided the excuse and the war still raging in 1944 certainly contributed. To my young unsophisticated mind, I saw all the future opportunities were there to be grasped outside the school system. I saw the Grammar School as an alien institution filled with students from owner occupied houses. The Technical School seemed unattractively full of teachers who looked for all the world like machine shop foremen.

On reflection I wonder at the stupidity of my determination to throw myself into the deep end of industrial life —and a very deep end it turned out to be.

I entered the joiner's shop in the GEC factory in Swinton and life there provided the first steps in craftsmanship, together with a few other hesitant lessons in life. My mentor in the joiner's shop was a fine craftsman of the old school who guided me through the first stages, in which I acquired some elementary skill. At an early date I was taken through the traditional task of building a toolbox for myself. The protocol demanded lessons in constructing dovetail joints and in finishing the wood down to the required width. I still possess the toolbox some 50 years later—though I honestly cannot say that I look at it with any pride. I had other tasks pressed upon me in my early days in 'the workshop'. I made a mallet and constructed the body of a wooden smoothing plane. When I now wander around antique shows and see, listed as antiques, tools of the kind I constructed as an apprentice, I feel my age.

The GEC factory was sloppily managed, with little formal discipline imposed. I soon learned that the whole factory could be explored at will and without challenge, every department stopped at and every attractive girl visited, so long as I carried a few sheets of official looking paper. The woodworking shop had many periods of low pressure, so my forays into the excitement of the production lines were fairly frequent and I developed a familiar relationship with people—especially the ladies—in each of the production departments.

By the end of 1944 the allied victory against Germany had lowered the physical tension of war in this country but it had released an intense emotional urge to celebrate. Christmas 1944 in that factory provided the excuse for a celebration, which turned the production lines into a wild drunken feast. With my 'official' bits of paper I set off to explore this behaviour first hand. In the end I had to run for my life in front of various posses of females who yelled all kinds of promises of action they would take, should they catch me. I ran fast in those days.

By early 1945 the War Department cut back on its orders for new aircraft. The war with Japan came to its violent conclusion as the experiments in Los Alamos were extended to Hiroshima and Nagasaki. The Swinton factory shed its labour and I faced my first redundancy before I had reached the age of 15.

The Woodworkers' Union ran a fairly effective information service so within three or four days I continued my apprenticeship with a cabinet maker / funeral director and jobbing builder. The workshop had few mechanical aids apart from a planing machine and a circular saw. In consequence all the hardwood for the furniture or the coffins had to be cut and finished by hand; a long and tedious labour. Yet it was an exercise, which, in its repetition, encouraged the development of skills that stood me well in the years ahead.

About this time I began to read again. I enrolled in an evening class at my old school to study English Literature and under some loose guidance began both to read and to write. My friends and work colleagues regarded this exercise as distinctly odd! I should, in their view, have been engaged in technical studies.

Despite my tutor's effort, my readings tended to be governed by caprice and prejudice and I flashed from one point on the literary spectrum to the other. Of course I absorbed the standard left wing texts—*The Ragged Trousered Philanthropist*; every text of George Bernard Shaw's work I could obtain, various novels by Maxim

Gorki and a few works by H G Wells. But I also found an appreciation for Rudyard Kipling and was so captivated by a gifted book of short stories by Damon Runyon, *Blue Plate Special*, that I recall reading it three times through without a break. There were many other volumes—some rejected when the language and concepts assumed more than I could bring to the interpretation. But I managed to struggle through some Wordsworth poems and a few novels by D H Lawrence.

IMPRESSIONS

It was around this period that a visual image had an impact upon me, which so indelibly marked my consciousness that I carry the emotional response to this day. The image of the Holocaust, which I saw on the flickering screen of a Pathe Pictoral Newsreel at the Majestic Cinema, so disturbed my 15-year-old stomach that I had to retreat to the toilet. I do not remember if I managed to sit through the main film, but I do know that the black and white images of the bodies dressed in stripes, piled high with the topmost still slightly moving, have remained in my mind's eye ever since.

That impact of the brutality of man was later replicated in another context. I read John Hersey's book *Hiroshima* soon after its publication. In his book he records the horror of the atomic bomb explosion on that City in 1945. To the point of reading, I admit that, in my conditioned mind the Japanese were not high on my list of species to be preserved. When the two atomic bombs were detonated over the Japanese cities I responded, as any young nationalist would do—with loud cheers. In Hersey's book I had to deal with the brutality of a bomb which killed and mutilated thousands of civilised and sophisticated men, women and children and continued its destruction of lives over the following generations.

As men and women from the forces returned home from the war—the newly elected Labour government, both representing and being charged with the increasing aspirations of the voters—set about the immense task of post-war reconstruction. The building industry formed a central plank in the government's regeneration programme and it soon became apparent that it provided some useful jobs opportunities. From my youthful and inexperienced viewpoint the industry seemed to offer a variety of work and companionship, with fresh air as a bonus. Naturally I never foresaw the ferocious winters to come.

I joined a scheme organised to train apprentices in the skills of the construction industry. Around thirty teenage apprentices worked on the scheme under adult supervision and were charged with the task of completing the construction of twenty houses. We drove the supervisors to distraction with our games, but eventually completed the task and the houses still stand and, I presume, house twenty families.

SHAKING LOOSE

In the 1970s, unemployment brought economic ruin to most of the industrial working class communities in Britain. Coal mining communities were particularly badly affected.

Not that these were areas of affluence in the 1940s and 1950s. Coal miners were at the head of the manual worker income scale in the 1950s but their traditional lifestyle provided little in the way of luxury.

In the post war period, the town of my birth had little culture; no music beyond the annual Handel's *Messiah*, no theatre but for an occasional visiting repertory company, no art and its architecture uniformly dull. But, thanks to Mr Carnegie, it had a sparsely stocked though well used library, in which I spent considerable time.

In South Wales the mining villages were vital communities. Miners' welfare centres housed lively activity and debate. Many of the South Wales collieries had leisure centres with well stocked libraries which fed the intellectual and political appetites of the miners. Oddly, when in the 1920s depression the South Wales miners tramped north to the still working Yorkshire coalfields, they brought with them little of that Welsh nurtured appetite for knowledge, music and debate.

In the 1940s and 50s my home town was a dead centre —stifling in its conformity. The predominant social pressure flattened the aspirations of the bright, mocked any deviation from the acceptable mundane. The downward social pressure protected the sensitivities of the majority, who subconsciously recognised that in all probability, they were sentenced by fate, or sod's law, to spend the rest of their lives in the boredom of that depressing place.

It was not easy to break out, but some notable characters had done so: a founder of the Canadian Social Credit Party, a leading Grand Prix racing driver, a subsequently wealthy television writer. But the act of leaving required purpose, effective process, money and determination.

That last vital quality I drew in abundance from my mother, together with her full encouragement for my purpose. Throughout her life she longed to leave that place, but sadly, (apart from some gloriously enjoyable holidays) she never managed to do so.

I inherited a restless nature from my mother and I constantly played with schemes to change occupation, or move town, or even to emigrate. I eventually worked the emigration prospect, with the strong support of my mother, to within a hair's breadth of moving to Canada. I stayed with the familiar life, in the expectation that I could be on my way to a parliamentary seat.

STEPPING OUT

Reaching the age of maturity at 21 meant more than the achievement of a skilled qualification; it led in the 1950s to a two-year detachment to the military as a National Service recruit. It was a prospect that held no attractions, despite my ambition to be on the move.

Before I took on the mould breaking experience of military service I travelled with a friend to Belgium, making my first journey abroad. We went by boat from Immingham to Ghent staying with a generous cafe proprietor in that city who had been friends of the family before the war. We spent an interesting week there before accompanying our hosts on their vacation, camping in the village of Echternach in Luxembourg.

For Belgium, a country divided by religion and language, this was a particularly disturbing period and we found ourselves on vacation in the centre of a revolution.

The Cafe Louise, owned by our hosts, was located in the old dock area of Ghent but had plenty of residential and some retirement homes around it. The cafe next door employed a pretty girl who worked as a prostitute, with whom we spent many hours in earnest conversation; though neither my friend nor I had enough of a grasp of the Flemish language to take the conversation very far.

Opposite the cafe a multi-coloured stone wall ran half the length of the street. We were shown, one evening, some peculiar chips and indentations in clusters along the wall. I had made some juvenile comment about the German occupation and in response some of the cafe clientele took us outside to show the bullet marks sculptured in the wall through its use by a firing squad in the early years of the occupation. One cafe client had seen his brother shot; another had seen his best friend destroyed there. I was amazed that they still came to the Cafe Louise to sit, talk and drink their Stella beers as though it were simply a recreational place beyond the reach of the tensions and problems of their daily lives.

After a week we departed from the Cafe Louise and headed for Luxembourg in Frank's Citroen piled high with camping equipment. The low-slung black Citroen induced in the two immature British minds the vision of the Gestapo; we played the game from the backseats of the car, all the way to Echternach to the consternation of our generous hosts.

It was an idyllic holiday, the weather as always in memory, is now remembered as hot and conducive to outdoor adventure. We talked to anyone who looked to be in any way responsive. We traded upon our curiosity value —the British were not then travelling—and we made many friends. After chatting to an attractive girl cycling from the shops we were repeatedly invited to visit the family of a Count on the edge of town. The family obviously delighted in the English conversation. We grew tired of the exercise when we recognised that our effort was taking us no nearer the attractive granddaughter.

Many years later I took my whole family, Geraldine, Steven and Alyce on a camping holiday in Echternach. One evening, Geraldine, following my eye roving over an attractive occupant of a neighbouring tent, observed that she could well be the daughter of the beauty I pursued on my previous visit. How dispiriting!

On that first youthful visit, just before we packed the tent for our return to Ghent, the campsite seemed to generate an unusual level of agitated discussion between the campers. A plane passing over the campsite, followed by two military planes, caused some sharp discussion and friction between people on the site.

King Leopold had declared his intention to return to Belgium and claim the Belgian throne. The quality of his relations with the German military during the occupation had been widely interpreted by many in Belgium as collaboration and a wide body of opinion opposed his return. The natural fracture in Belgian society between Walloon and the Flemish began to widen.

On our return we set off on our journey from Luxembourg to Ghent planning to stop for a meal in Brussels. News on a radio before we left told of a march to Brussels initiated by a modest hundred or so opponents of Leopold. We had problems entering the capital city and circled around the outskirts, finally entering alongside a stream of marchers estimated at 500,000 strong. As we entered the city, searching for a quiet place to eat we realised that Brussels was already occupied by Leopold's opponents. I have a memory of a cortege of flowers on its way to the

Palace donated by an order of nuns, being overturned in the square in which we had settled for our lunch. We made a rapid departure.

We finally arrived in Ghent to discover the docks immobilised by a general strike and our journey home to England put in jeopardy.

Leopold finally abdicated in 1951 in favour of his rather unambitious but diplomatically skilful son following a national referendum on the monarchy. To his great credit Baudouin made a crucial contribution to the unity of his fractious nation over the 42 years of his eventual reign. As I write this text the daily newspapers are reporting his death and from all political sides they report the wide respect of his people.

MINIMALIST MILITARY

July 1951 I completed my apprenticeship as a carpenter and joiner and then received instructions to report for military duty to RAF Padgate for basic training or 'square bashing' as it is more accurately described. It proved to be the usual mindless process of confinement to camp for seven weeks of parade ground drill, during which the non-commissioned officers yelled at us in an impossible attempt to remould our determinedly free spirits to fit the needs of the military.

On the second weekend, the boredom of another Saturday afternoon and Sunday confined to the camp was persuasive enough to see me through a gap in the fence and past the outside guardroom to spend a welcoming weekend at home. I thereby began my military service as I was to continue it for the following two years; escaping at every available opportunity.

Following Padgate a complement of 36 recruits, all time served and skilled woodworkers, were despatched to St Athen airbase. An unfortunate corporal, with little more than 10 weeks training in the skills of woodcraft was detailed to instruct us in the basic elements of the craft. To his credit he quickly responded to the challenge and, abandoning the original programme, he channelled our talents into the construction of a yacht for the RAF St Athan sailing club. That task occupied virtually all the sixteen weeks training period, following which we were posted to our service stations.

A longstanding friend and I had attended together the military pre-service assessment and medical tests. He chose to nominate the Mountain Rescue as his preferred service option: I chose Air Sea Rescue. We should have reckoned with the perversity of the military mind, which saw me posted to Inverness and eventual attachment to the Mountain Rescue Team and his posting to the Southampton Air Sea Rescue Unit.

The Dalcross Camp, now Inverness airport, to which I was posted, had been closed since the end of the war and then reopened in response to the Korean conflict. We found it to be fairly primitive, though the small British Airways lounge offered some civilized relief once we won the favour of the friendly staff. On a few occasions I persuaded the crew of the BA Rapide biplanes to take me on their round trips to the islands. The plane schedules were frequently governed by the tides, landing as they did on the beach.

At Dalcross I joined with a colleague, Major Platt, to form the Dalcross Music Society and with a generous grant of funds from the education officer we set out to purchase a range of recordings to suit our taste. I cannot recall any other participants for the many winter evenings we spent with the music. For my part I fed on Major's extensive musical knowledge.

Apart from the musical evenings, the treks into the mountains with the Kinloss Mountain Rescue Team, and independent weekends exploring the magnificent scenery, my main occupation seems to have been the exploration of schemes to legitimately detach myself from the camp. I developed a friendship with a pilot who by chance had a girlfriend in Doncaster. Many weekends we flew to the town returning back early Monday morning.

I then found the provisions of the educational service to be of assistance and enjoyed two separate 14-day detachments to Nottingham University. It was during this time that I determined the need to return to full-time education.

Having taken two programmes at the university, that educational avenue of escape from the camp routine was blocked by some regulation, so other means had to be discovered. I sought freedom through physical adventure; but I should have known better. Volunteering for parachute training I found may bring release from daily routine, but it substitutes a ritual, which threatens death if the ritual is ignored. I jumped—or to be strictly accurate I was thrust—from the plane by a corporal. I did not take kindly to the experience.

Jumping provided another military experience and from a far less dramatic height it almost saw the end of me. On a weekend, with no prospect of a free flight to Doncaster, I purchased an unwanted travel warrant from a colleague. The journey by train had few problems from Inverness to Edinburgh apart from the tediously slow pace. At Edinburgh, late in the day, I boarded a London bound train only to find, as we left Darlington, that the train had no scheduled stop before London. The train passed through York at high speed and promised an equally rapid track through Doncaster. I was foolishly desperate having no money and too little time left in the weekend to travel to and from London. As the train whipped through Doncaster station, its brakes were applied to slow down, in deference to a well-remembered train crash on a bend by the bridges beyond the station. The braking and total darkness led me into a false sense of the actual speed and, after gaining the complicity of a fellow passenger to close the door behind me, I launched myself from the train into a black void. As I let go I realised the stupidity of my action—I floated through the air and hit the ground very hard. I came round with a railway lamp in my eyes and a railway worker shaking me into sensibility. He pulled my limp legs from the track across which I fallen with urgent shouts to move before a train came roaring along that very line. My uniform persuaded the railway worker to allow me to limp away without reporting the event to his superiors. Following that foolish event I spent the best part of a week in hospital with an injured foot. On return to the camp, despite my best endeavours my plastered leg and other bruising gained no sympathy. 'Injured alighting from a train lad', questioned the duty officer, 'and how fast would that train be going at the time?' I spent a week confined to punishment duties—but my injuries and limp ensured that the duties were fairly light.

My two-year National Service typically came to a close during an absence from the camp. One evening I began to suffer increasing pain in the gut. At some time after midnight I staggered to the guardroom and demanded attention.

Laid out in Inverness hospital, recovering from an appendectomy was not the way I had planned to celebrate my demobilisation. It was anything but keyhole surgery, and on my return home my father felt it appropriate to arrange for me to stay for a couple of weeks with an old colleague, Harry Dark and his wife in Jersey. Harry had worked throughout the war and German occupation on the island and had many stories to tell of some of his and his friends' subversive activities. He impressed upon me the need to make firm plans for my future. He urged that I should go back to school. He warned that if I failed to be decisive then events would conspire to subvert my ambition. When I returned from Jersey I knew where I intended to go.

Before I could realise the future I returned to hard labour in the construction industry to accumulate the money I needed for a period at college.

Two The Breakout

In the summer of 1956 I made a journey to Finland to join the summer camp of the International Union of Socialist Youth. The journey to Tampere took us by train through Germany and Denmark across the ferry to Gothenberg. From Stockholm the overnight journey to Finland had a magical air. We laid in sleeping bags on deck with the late June sun sitting on the horizon lighting all the archipelago islands into various shades of pink. At the camp in Tampere the long daylight hours raised a problem. After hours of sport, debate, singing and social intercourse the sun would finally dip below the trees across the lake: but within the hour the light would change its quality as the sun began its ascent and the damned birds began their dawn chorus. Tents I discovered are far from sound-proofed.

Though the camp participants were drawn from Europe and Scandinavia, we discovered some friendly fellows with American accents. They were dressed casually but somewhat unfitted for camping. American government policy, at that time, strongly favoured a greater political unity in Europe and the democratic socialist movements in the various Western European nations were in line with that desire. They were also, for the most part strongly anti-Communist and this too found favour in Washington.

The British contingent on the camp—as always— arrived with no uniformed shirts, no shorts, no football boots or other sporting gear. We needed to face up with style to the challenge of the Germans in a sporting competition. I prevailed upon our American colleagues—who admitted that they were there to foster good relations— to fund the purchase of football gear for the British team. The cash came in a roll of notes: the only condition being my agreement to sign a US Government headed financial receipt! We lost the game—but as always we were sporting losers.

At the finale of the Finnish camp the programme promised a grand march of all the national delegations to take place before invited dignitaries from the host city, culminating in a grand concert on the shore of the lake at sundown.

The German delegation, mainly from the Falcon movement, were dressed in smart uniforms which to our prejudiced British eyes looked too much like the recently discarded outfits of Hitler League of Youth. They also sported a range of colourful pennants on poles, which gave them the appearance of a well-drilled and efficiently organised group. By contrast the British were dressed in a motley and rather shabby attire and a Union Jack for a parade would have been the last thing any of us would have thought to bring to Finland. We thought to make one—but on the edge of abandoning the idea I decided to call on the British Consul in Tampere. He was a charming fellow—married as I recall to a Finnish lady and delighted to loan a flag or two to such patriotic chaps! I asked him what had happened to the Consulate Office during the war —conscious of the fact that following the Soviet attack on that tiny country Finland had lined itself with Germany during the rest of the war. The Consul looked surprised by the question, 'nothing had happened', he said, he had remained throughout as Consul. What about the flag flying outside his Consular home I asked. It flew there throughout the whole of the war he proudly maintained.

I never did check out that story with the Foreign Office —but prefer in any case to believe it.

On my train journey back from Finland I occupied the hours with Steinbeck's *Grapes of Wrath* and determined that, like the 'Okies', I would pack my bags and depart from my previous lifestyle.

COLLEGE ON A SHOESTRING

In 1956 Fircroft College was still run with that sense of idealism which had inspired George Cadbury to establish the institution. He did so after one of his visits to Denmark had allowed him to see a Danish Folk High School at work. The Principal, an intellectual and saintly fellow called Leslie Stephens ran the college with a total conviction that the adult students would be socially and intellectually transformed by their one year's experience. I wrote to him on my return from Finland to ask if I could apply, at that late stage, for a place in the coming academic year. I was accepted and applied to the county authority for a grant towards the fees. The interview panel at the county had a blunt Yorkshire businessman in the chair and a jolly Labour councillor who unfortunately encouraged my exasperation at the stupidity of the questions and comments. The final questions and display of ignorance from the panel encouraged me, foolishly, to issue a sharp rebuke. 'Do you read lad?' asked the chairman. 'Yes sir', I replied. 'And what are you reading now?' he asked. I told him that I had just completed Steinbeck's *Grapes of Wrath*. 'Is he an American?' he asked. The whole line of questioning had already indicated a total lack of sympathy with my ambition. So I replied that it was not for me to advise them of such a fact when they were the ones charged to judge me.

The letter from the county I retained for many years. It said that the majority of the committee judged me to be 'not yet mature enough to warrant a grant'. I was then 26 years of age.

Leslie Stephens urged that I should not be deterred and he managed to find a small amount of money to cover the fees. It was with great joy and anticipation that I boarded the train for Birmingham and then by bus to Bournville. The college enrolled only 36 students so we enjoyed the luxury of almost personal guidance throughout our studies. That year the college moved into George Cadbury's fine house bequeathed to it in his will and I left my mark there, returning to build fittings and furnishings in vacations over the next year.

It was in Bournville that I met Geraldine, felt a compelling attraction and rashly asked her to marry me. I have never for a moment doubted the wisdom of that decision but I can only speak for my part of that enduring union. We met 'romantically' in a gas show room doorway on a blind date organised by a friend. A year later I sent a card to Geraldine with the following bad verse inside:

> Love, a most discerning bard once said,
> Will walk where wise men fear to tread
> But never told us how we're drawn
> Into that foolish state forlorn
> Oh! that I had some such warning
> On a certain rainy morning
> Bachelorhood—thy noble freedom's tomb
> Sealed in the door of a gas show room
>
> So let me warn you, dodgers of the cherubs dart
> 'Tis not just cupid who can spear the heart
> Since one short year ago, I lay infirm
> A victim to that heater—Mr Therm!

Following Fircroft I moved my studies to Ruskin College Oxford. In some ways that move signified a temporary lack of confidence: I should have gone with the opportunity and taken an available place at the University of Keele. But Ruskin had been in mind over the years and it seemed to offer a more 'classical' education for an aspiring candidate of the left than a provincial university. Mistake or not it proved to be a formative and stimulating two years and a period in which we established some enduring friendships.

For the two years in Oxford we rented a caravan in the grounds of the Bickfords' house in Forest Hill. Whilst I grafted away on essays and in pushing back the frontiers of my knowledge my new wife worked to keep us. Again our grant was too small, deliberately not recognising my married status.

The financial crisis came to a head during the stress of the final examinations. In a perfectly timed bit of family planning Geraldine lay in the Churchill Hospital in the final stages of labour. Between visits I tried to mug-up some of the detail for the papers faced each day in the schools. In the midst of this drama the Calor Gas ran out—we had literally no food in the larder and the last few shillings from my final student cheque had drained away. This was real trouble and I refused to turn again to my parents following their past generosity. In desperation I wrote to the Woodworkers' Union General Secretary to describe my plight. It must have been a convincing letter. By return post he sent a £50 cheque which allowed us to survive until my mother skilfully organised our rescue from Oxford.

That gesture by the Woodworkers' Union might seem little, but it was so immediate and unconditional that I determined to pay back their generosity. Though no longer involved in the craft of the industry I continued my membership of the union until their grant had been returned with interest. Indeed many years later, the re-doubtable Clive Jenkins publicly described me as the only member of a TUC affiliated union ever to have served in the Diplomatic Service. It is a record which must surely have been surpassed with the affiliation into the TUC of the First Division Association.

So much for the drama and hardship; but what of the academic study? I took the opportunity to sit, always capti-vated, through as many lectures by A J P Taylor as I could fit into the timetable, attended a number of sessions by Isaiah Berlin and participated in the formative seminars conducted at Nuffield by Alan Flanders and Hugh Clegg. It was at one of these seminars that I brashly set out to take apart the thesis presented by the very young but clearly intellectually challenging Peter Jay. Luckily he had forgotten the face, if not the event when it came to my interview with Ambassador Jay in the Foreign Office prior to my Washington appointment.

In the industrial relations part of the study I faced some tough opposition from my tutor for challenging the then orthodox Ruskin view of collective bargaining as a political expression of working class solidarity. My politically incorrect essays, influenced by the works of John Dunlop, were returned with as much comment written into them by my tutor as they had in original text by me.

Having completed the Diploma in Politics and Economics (Dip Pol Econ Oxon) I should have stayed in Oxford to continue for the degree and Balliol seemed sympathetic to that ambition. The struggle to persuade the authorities to provide another grant seemed hopeless. With a son as well as a wife our financial plight was desperate so a teaching course with its secure funding seemed the best option. I continued to regret that choice for some years.

Following our rescue from Oxford we spent another year surviving, this time in London, where I qualified to teach. The course was facile but the economic struggle to complete it provided real drama to the year. The college at the Elephant and Castle was housed in an old workhouse —a fact that my wife and I found to be entirely appropriate in our financial circumstances. We ate the basic necessities, walked everywhere, pushing Steve for miles in the family donated pram and our ill-fitting clothes were cast offs from the family; except for Steve who was dressed like a prince by his grandparents.

I frequently walked all the way to college from the Forest Hill area of South London where we lived to save the bus fare. I took to eating lunch in a white tile cafe which seemed to cater for the homeless. I found that I could dine on two scoops of potatoes for two pence and have the luxury of parsley sauce for an extra penny.

None of this seemed to be too bad at the time for we knew it would not last. I had determined that, in good time I would sit in the House of Commons complete with striped trousers, maroon tie and matching socks and be charged by my constituents to take forward the radical changes needed to both increase our national wealth and to ensure its equitable distribution!

I had, with all seriousness, thought through where I would wish to make a political contribution and that would be in housing policy. It seemed to me then that both major political parties brought stereotype phrases rather than policy into their approach to housing. There continues to be a strong element of truth in that view and no government in those intervening years has brought with it any comprehensive strategy which integrates housing into its other economic and social policies.

FROM HULL, HELL AND HALIFAX ...

From the London year I had to find a job in teaching. I owed the banks a large amount of money borrowed to see us through the four 'indulgent' college years. The solution to the linked needs of job and house seemed to be a teaching job in a town so short of teaching talent that a house would be provided as a recruiting inducement. For good or ill that decision led to a teaching post at the Further Education College in Halifax which came with a pretty depressing flat on a windswept hill on the outskirts of town. We had no furniture—not even a bed to furnish the flat. My mother organised a furniture removal van, provided a deposit for a couch which doubled as a bed and she instructed the removal men to clear out for us all the furniture from the whole ground floor of her house. God only knows what my father said when he returned from work to find the place completely bare. My mother simply waved us off with the cheery view that she had tried all ways to get new furniture and generosity was simply her ultimate sanction in her bid for something new.

The Halifax job proved to be hard graft with little compensation. I formed a Fabian Group in town and we enjoyed a few evenings with Edward Thompson—then in the midst of writing his classic Making of the English Working Classes. In the run-up to the general election of 1964 I organised town meetings, factory gate meetings and visits to social clubs for the Labour Candidate Shirley Summerskill. The general election results were predictably close and Halifax gained considerable publicity with the contest between Maurice Macmillan, son of a Prime Minister and Shirley Summerskill, the daughter of a well known Labour Minister. Shirley emerged as a charming and intelligent candidate but unnervingly unsure when she had to meet with her potential supporters. I steered her around various events guiding her towards people she should meet, persuading her to shake hands with people and promoting opportunities for her to speak. At the same time Geraldine organised a series of coffee mornings hosted by ourselves or other active women and to these we invited only women we knew not to be actively engaged in politics.

I also organised a major eve of the poll conference at which George Brown was billed as the major speaker. He arrived late and hoarse from his hundreds of previous speaking engagements. Striding to the platform to loud applause—some of it in sheer relief at his eventual arrival—he yanked at the microphone to adjust it but instead pulled it from its socket. As he stared at the two pieces he exclaimed 'Good God I've made a mess of this'. His words broadcast across the hall. A bright young fellow in the front took the opportunity to yell the comment that it signified the mess Brown would make if he and his colleagues were returned to office. Brown then deftly slotted the microphone head back into its socket and responded that when he and his colleagues messed things up, they had the skill and good sense to know how to put matters right. I suspect that he had practised that trick at every stop in his campaign—never failing to draw out the waiting victim.

Our daughter Alyce was born in Halifax. It was a joyful occasion for all of us including young Steven who took such a pride in the event that one might have assumed he had achieved the creation of a sister single-handed. He was never jealous of the intrusion and wanted always to care for his sister. Alyce was born in the middle of the worst winter for years and we found the severity of the climate compounded by our elevated position, perched as we were high on a Pennine hill. As Geraldine began her labour pains I ran to a neighbour's phone to call an ambulance but with the road too treacherous for the vehicle to complete the last 200 yards up the hill she had to walk down to meet it.

With her return home with Alyce the great freeze softened a little and a recently installed heater on the top floor thawed out the main water pipe from its frozen and fractured state. We were deluged with a cascade of water, which effectively destroyed three apartments and their belongings, thankfully missing us by a whisker.

SHOP STEWARDS

At the college in Halifax I began one of the first day release courses for shop stewards to be run in the country. To put the programme in place I had to persuade the local engineering employers of its value and to engage the unions in the promotion of the course. It was no easy task but I was assisted by an agreement between the then British Employers Confederation and the TUC, which called for the widespread development of shop steward training. Beyond the far left rhetoric of class conflict and the arguments for industrial strife to improve working class power, it was painfully obvious that British industrial relations were bedevilled by a sheer lack of comprehension between the parties. They were literally schools apart; they were culturally separate. If a conflict of interest is inevitable between those at work and their employers, then at least it should be conflict conducted with clarity of understanding.

Some years later I visited the Employers Confederation in Sweden where they told me of a walk-out by the door-keepers in the building. The employer organisation provided the venue for the mediation of national disputes. As the employer or trade union officials arrived they needed to be steered to the confines of their separate rooms but convention had never allowed notices. The door-keepers had the task of judging into which group each arrival fitted. Finally the door-keepers walked out to protest against their impossible task. The parties looked alike, wore equally good suits, could not be distinguished by accent and even the newspapers they carried could not be used to distinguish them.

I recognise that it was a judgement in the context of a very different social system—but the search for solutions to Britain's chronic labour relations difficulties offered opportunity for various solutions and the Swedish system seemed then to be attractive. In truth Swedish collective bargaining was not all sweetness and light—some tough decisions had to be faced; but it seemed that their disputes were centred on matters of substance, less on major misunderstanding and were rarely based upon a sheer lack of trust arising from class incomprehension.

Our shop steward courses were not aimed at industrial tranquillity but on the effective working of agreed procedures: but it soon became apparent that disruptive misunderstanding arose from the fact that the agreed system was as much unwritten as it was written. The teaching material came from various sources. Apart from my own materials I received some interesting papers from Fred Hoehler, then teaching autoworkers in Michigan. He provided a number of ideas I adapted for our own programmes. In Oxford Arthur Marsh had developed a series of teaching documents linked to the engineering industry disputes procedures. He generously allowed me to go through his filing cabinets and, where two documents existed, I was permitted to take one.

THE OXFORD SCHOOL

For all this experimental work with unions and matching work with supervisors, I found Halifax to be a constricting and insular environment. A change of environment was needed to expand the work and, rather sadly, I concluded that the new environment would be in the South where it was possible to find a more liberal approach by the colleges and a greater response by the local employer associations.

In the summer of 1964 we moved south to Essex. The move coincided with a growing national concern for the disruptive nature of our collective bargaining system. The reconstituted employer organisation (the CBI) and the TUC were persuaded by the Labour government to work out the basis on which they would agree a policy to influence the movement of prices and incomes. Following an agreement on the basic principles they went on to decide the appropriate machinery for implementing that policy. By this jointly agreed approach the National Board for Prices and Incomes (NBPI) was established with the support and participation of all the major parties involved in collective bargaining. It was a process in which I was determined to play a part.

Major Oxford academics were recruited into various roles in the NBPI. Both Alan Flanders and Hugh Clegg had begun to establish the case for the reform of collective bargaining and the basis on which they believed those reforms should be promoted.

Flanders had established his thesis in his widely influential analysis of the Esso Fawley Productivity Agreement. In his view British industrial relations were bedevilled by two systems of collective bargaining, one existing in the mass of written and mainly archaic jointly agreed procedures and the other system within the informal conventions and practices which governed the effective behaviour, particularly at plant and workshop levels. I recall Flanders

illustrating his thesis with the example of a building industry shop steward whose role and function were unrecog-
nised in any of the written negotiating procedures or any
of the formally agreed rules. Yet the building industry
stewards existed in reality and were at that time powerful
figures in the determination of effective pay at site level. It
was no good, said Flanders, defining unconstitutional
action as being unacceptable in those circumstances. How,
he asked, could the building stewards abide by procedures
which denied their very existence? In Flanders' view we
needed to develop procedures which met the needs of the
parties and reflected their effective relationships. They
needed to be jointly agreed procedures and the two sides
then required to abide by the agreement.

The second strand of the Oxford thesis applied to payment systems, which in many industries had developed a
complexity which defied effective rational control. Many
pay systems were only tenuously linked to achievement
and in some industries—Fleet Street[1] at that time was an
example—the dynamics of a pay system owed more to the
interplay of shop floor power politics than to productivity, profit or the effective contribution of the workforce.

Soon after my appointment to the Essex College I was
pleased to be drawn into the NBPI's work as one of its
Industrial Relations Advisers. In that capacity, I worked
on a number of the major questions referred to the Board
by the Secretary of State. I conducted case studies in the
engineering industry, on collective bargaining procedures
in the building and construction industries and on various aspects of productivity bargaining which the Board

1. The National Newspapers were at that time housed in and around
Fleet Street.

sought to promote as a central part of its activity. I also worked on various general references and themes examined by the Board.

The NBPI in its early days looked to many as though it might succeed where other instruments of government had failed. With the retrospective gift of hindsight its inevitable failure is all too apparent. On the credit side the Board's research illustrated the wide-ranging problems with pay systems. Its reports continued to be influential for many years after the Board's demise and many thinking employers, consultants and academics involved in the reform of management and pay systems continued to draw on the evidence and distilled wisdom in the reports.

As a central instrument in a voluntary incomes policy the Board stood no chance of achieving long term success. When it came to effective control the Board found its functions swept aside by the 1966 sterling crisis which led the government to abandon voluntarism and to legislate against pay and price increases. One has to say—again in hindsight—that certain central assumptions underpinning the Board's functions had more than a little arrogance and elitism running through them. In broad terms the assumption that a small band of highly intelligent academics employed to illustrate the truth of pay systems can, by that process, effectively control them against the pressures of the labour market and the combined ingenuity of unions and employers—now looks both naive and hopeless. The real impact on pay came with the devaluation of sterling in 1967. With all the many economic problems facing the country it was an electoral wonder that Harold Wilson managed to convert his slender majority to the solid working majority in the 1966 election.

During this period I earned my principal income from the college in Essex where I headed the branch which promoted a whole series of part-time, residential and block release courses in labour relations. With my colleague George Healy I went to see Jack Jones, the Transport and general Workers' Union (T&GWU) General Secretary and won his agreement to take all the dockworker shop stewards through a basic training course. At that time of our meeting with him Jack had been in office only a few days; but with the bronze bust of Ernest Bevin looking over his shoulder he looked and behaved as though he had been there for a decade. He agreed to our proposition for the training programme but he saw to it that we began our intake of stewards with the whole of the No.1 Docks Group —which had the reputation of being the toughest and most battle hardened dock stewards in the business. We survived the experience and the programme ran its full course.

In the late 60s the docks were on the edge of massive changes. The causal basis of employment had been replaced with a basic wage under a general contract with the Dock Labour Board. Before the new employment security had time to effectively settle in, the industry began to experience radical changes in technology. The conventional method of shipping loose cargoes began to disappear and containerised cargoes were introduced backed in some cases by roll on and off methods of transportation. It was only a matter of time before the old labour practices were eliminated by the technological and system changes.

The work in Essex brought us into fairly close working relationships with most of the trade union leaders of the time. Vic Feather, first as Assistant then as General Secretary to the Trades Union Congress (TUC) was a strong supporter and a regular contributor. Clive Jenkins appeared on a number of occasions and Alan Fisher, General Secretary of National Union of Public Employers (NUPE) gave many sessions linked into our programmes. We also sought to introduce occasional controversy from outside the union ranks. Enoch Powell attended and outlined a thesis to prove that, in the longer-term, unions have no effect on the real level of earnings. A fair number of employers also made regular contributions. These broader educational sessions were peripheral to the central objectives of most courses that aimed primarily to improve the knowledge and the bargaining techniques of the participants.

At one point we proposed to open the programmes to an occasional overseas experience. Already the docks stewards had visited Rotterdam to see the effects of fully containerised and computerised cargoes. To widen this overseas experience I wrote to a number of union federations overseas to see if any wished to establish reciprocal visits on mutually agreed training programmes. The Swedish Labour Organisation proved keen and we had exchanges that ran for some years. Early in 1968 I had a letter from the French CGT Union Federation which proposed that their education officials visit the College to hold discussions on a possible exchange. The letter caused a few problems—the CGT having its established traditional political base in the French Communist Party. The TUC said, 'go ahead but don't formally tell us'. I was keen for a number of reasons: for a start the CGT seemed to be an effective union force in France: it had a strong membership in the automobile industry and its perspective on events promised to be challenging.

In return for the CGT's exploratory visit I was invited to Paris to see their facilities and to pursue the difficult issue of the programme for the exchange. It was May 1968 with Paris in the grip of the student revolt. My hosts were CGT officials and I had no doubts as to their political affiliations. They met me at Beauvais airport and on the journey into Paris they corrected one major misconception on my part by fiercely denouncing the student revolt as the work of middle class 'Gauchists'.

Paris, in that May and June, was a divided city both geographically and across the age barriers. In one part of the city the cafes remained full and the conversations seemed as they always were. Cross a few streets and the tension was extreme. Everywhere the garbage mounted and public transport was virtually non-existent. At my foolish request the CGT officials took me to the Sorbonne where, in a nearby square, students stood in groups in each case with an older figure in their midst. The tutors were apparently seeking to cool tempers and to pacify the students. Suddenly from our vantage point in a cafe we saw that the square had been ringed by helmeted riot police clustered into vans. The police moved out of the vans, formed ranks, pulled down visors and moved into the square from all sides. My host yelled and we sprinted for our car a few yards away as the police swept through the square like a double blue wave, one rank behind the other. One fierce fellow began to beat the roof of our car with his baton and at the behest of my host I pressed my passport to the window and yelled 'tourist'. He waived us through. As we left the square I turned to witness the students undergoing some pretty rough treatment. Within a few hours some 20,000 students were on the streets, digging up cobbles, and fighting a pitched battle with the police.

By coincidence my principal host for the visit had an undergraduate son at the Sorbonne and active in the revolt. The father strongly denounced his son's activities, but to pacify the curiosity of a visiting Englishman he arranged through the son's contacts for us to meet with some of the student leaders. I was sorry to miss the opportunity to meet Daniel Cohn Bendit but I did get to talk to Alain Geismar and Jacques Sauvageot. During another trip across town I was taken on a surprise visit to the Folies Bergere theatre where all the performers were on strike and occupying the theatre. I made the awful comment to a group of the ladies that theirs was the only strike which entailed putting on clothes.

We also called in to see the clandestine publicity centre organised by the students to support their campaign. At that time the main French television stations had a practice of rating programmes judged unsuitable for children by indicating a little box in the left corner of the screen. Amongst the many remarkably striking posters hanging up to dry, like washing on a line, one poster had a pointed impact. It had no words—just a cartoon of General de Gaul with a small box in his mouth.

A few weeks after my visit to Paris the Gaulist Party were returned to office winning a massive victory in the French elections and the whole student revolt seemed a lost cause. In fact, against the wishes of his Prime Minister, the President set about the introduction of significant and wide ranging reforms of the French higher educational system, which few of the students I met during my visit would have believed possible under that Presidency.

Three Donovan and After

The year of my visit to Paris also saw the publication of the Royal Commission's report on trade unions and employers' associations—commonly called the Donovan Report. The Commission had worked on its study for three years and its research reports, published at intervals, had provided useful teaching material. Alan Flanders' evidence to the Commission in which he propounded his theory of the two systems of collective bargaining, the formal and the informal, became the central thesis of the Donovan report itself. From that base the Commission rejected propositions for the introduction of various legal provisions and sanctions to limit and contain strikes. Instead it called for a substantial reform of the system through voluntary agreements.

The Commission went on to recommend the registration of all major collective agreements and for a permanent Commission with access to the agreements and with the responsibility to negotiate reforms.

The Donovan recommendations were accepted by the

Labour government but in addition the government attempted to give itself some reserve legal powers to be held by the Secretary of State.

The Commission on Industrial Relations (CIR), established the year after the Donovan publication, had George Woodcock, recently retired General Secretary of the TUC, as its chairman and Alan Flanders as one of it board members. The Commission took on the task of promoting radical changes in collective bargaining structures by subjecting a single company or an entire industry to a thorough and detailed study and from that to establishing general principles. The Commission also had responsibility for determining union recognition cases, but without the legal authority to enforce its recognition decisions.

Soon after the CIR had been established I had a call from the Secretary to the Commission, Norman Singleton, to ask if I would be willing to see him in his office—and if convenient that very afternoon. I burdened my teaching colleagues with my classes and with excitement caught the train to London.

I remember some searching but typically polite questions from Norman who concluded with two questions —do you want to join us and when can you start? The Commission expected to be buried under references from the Secretary of State, Barbara Castle and its staff needed to be in place to take charge of them. I went back to college, negotiated my release with the help of a generous principal and three days later I joined the CIR.

My second day at the Commission proved to be a day of some considerable external excitement. From my office I looked out on a massive trade union demonstration winding its way along Kingsway in opposition to the

Labour government's proposition to provide for itself the reserve legal powers which it had proposed in its cutely entitled White Paper, *In Place of Strife*.

The deluge of references from the Secretary of State never materialised. The spirit of voluntarism extolled by Donovan had translated into the principle that any reference to the CIR should be first approved by both the TUC and the Confederation of British Industry (CBI). For a long period both sides effectively prevaricated on all cases. The high expectations built around the CIR's birth began to ebb away as it lay dormant for almost four months.

When the references finally came through, we employed many of the skills developed in the previous work with the NBPI. An inquiry into a company required a thorough and systematic analysis of the informal and formal bargaining arrangements, the details and the actual dynamics of the payments systems, the power structures and responsibilities in management and workforce, together with a clear understanding of the production and technology in the company.

My first task took me into a chemical company, Associated Octel, to head an inquiry into the plant where a union recognition demand had challenged management's historical belief that 'supervisors were part of management and management did not join unions'. The company was not obstructive to our inquiry but they did not regard the Commission as being objective. We were not in the business of pushing people into collective bargaining but we nonetheless drew our general presumptions from Donovan—that collective bargaining was the best means of regulating the terms of employment. With that presumption and in the context of its time, it was highly unlikely that the Commission would find against a workgroup claiming collective bargaining rights. The International Harvester inquiry offered another kind of challenge. The two factories in Doncaster and one in Bradford had suffered a constant and high level of conflict. I led a talented team sent in by the Commission and we virtually lived in the factories for seven months putting both systems and behaviour through a rigorous analysis. Finally we recommended substantial changes to the pay system; designed a new procedure and negotiated it into agreement with all parties. The whole process, strongly supported by the local MP Harold Walker[2], was one of the Commission's most successful cases. Of all CIR's work, the Harvester case probably came nearer to proving the central contention of the Donovan Commission and demonstrating the potential of the CIR procedures.

In that early period of the CIR we enjoyed a good working relationship with the top union leadership. As the references came through we had the need to meet most of the union leaders and they generally supported our activity.

On two references we had the interesting experience of dealing with Reg Birch, a national official of the Engineering Union. Reg was a total romantic in his politics and a perfect gentleman in his personal behaviour. He would assiduously walk around the table to shake hands with everyone at the commencement of a meeting and insist on repeating the procedure at the conclusion regardless of the numbers involved. In the meeting he brought a sharp experience to bear on issues and a skilful defence of his members' interests.

2. Appointed Minister of State at Employment Department, then Deputy Speaker and went finally to the Lords.

Along with most of his fellow communists Reg felt politically disorientated by the impact of Russian 'glasnost' on the world communist movement. He centred his attention on China and founded the 1968 offshoot Communist Party of Great Britain Marxist-Leninist, and served as its first chairman. At one of our meetings he offered sincere apologies for his inability to attend a sequential meeting, with the explanation that he had a visit to China planned for that time. As we left the meeting room I quipped that he should give my very best regards to Mao Tsetung. He politely called me back and solemnly explained that he understood Mao to be seriously ill and that on this occasion he would be unable to convey my regards.

I subsequently learned that Reg did indeed have access to the very highest level in the Chinese hierarchy.

It was around this time that Reg involved in an event at the Ford Motor Company that is now established in the anecdotal history of collective bargaining. With colleagues he attended a meeting at the company to hear of proposed changes to the employment conditions. The union representatives were submitted to a long and stiflingly boring presentation on pension benefits during which a repeated knocking occurred, presumably from the door. An inspection by a junior manager ascertained that no one stood outside. The presentation started again and once more the knocking began. After another repeat performance a manager saw Reg with his fist below the table and asked if he had a point to make. 'No', said Reg, 'it's not me. But it is my members who have passed away since this boring session began, wanting to know if these benefits are retrospective'.

I once asked Reg what he did at weekends. He said that

he looked through all his newspapers and news sheets to discover what demonstrations were planned. Then he would spend a long time in debate with family and friends deciding which side to support.

He was a determined, committed and wonderfully humorous man.

THE RIGHT RETURN

The General Election of 1970 brought a Conservative government to power with a commitment to introduce a body of labour law as the basis for a wide-ranging reform of industrial relations. Under Geoffrey Howe's guidance, the Act of 1971 brought in a complex of inter-related legal provisions which owed much to United State's labour law. Within the 1971 Act the CIR continued its broad reforming role and retained much of its voluntarist approach. It continued to retain its presumptions about the efficacy of collective bargaining, but it was charged to receive its recognition cases from the newly established Industrial Relations Court under its senior judge Sir John (later Lord) Donaldson. George Woodcock resigned from the Commission with other union official board members. Many of the staff with union backgrounds quickly found other jobs.

I had arranged with George Woodcock for him to speak to a major conference in Thurrock organised by my colleague George Healy. The arrangements had been made well before the unforeseen election so I found myself travelling with Woodcock to Essex. The occasion was set against the background of the newly proposed 1971 legislation already spelled out by the government in outline, together with the proposal to engage the CIR in the legal process.

George was a taciturn man at the best of times but that evening he was a gloomy as the night outside the car. He told me of his earlier conviction that the Commission could have radically changed our industrial relations practices but that public patience had run out. It was no good just blaming the press—the unions had to shoulder the blame for their failure to convince the broader public of their legitimacy. He said that I should stay with the Commission—it would be a difficult period and the unions would not be able to avoid the Act. They would need a sympathetic 'ear' inside the system and they would unofficially use it.

I had known George Woodcock for some years. He was a regular visitor to Ruskin during my time there and had interviewed me for a job at the TUC, which thankfully he determined, was not for me.

Woodcock had a powerful intellect, which enabled him to grasp the wider implications of events. That night he was a deeply saddened man and from the platform, as he concluded his speech, he announced his inevitable decision to resign from the chairmanship of the CIR.

The new Act had broken the basic contention of the British Unions—namely that the voluntary system of collective bargaining was the best and fairest possible system and that any body of law would by necessity and by tradition prove to be punitive for the unions.

There were many aspects of the 1971 Act that I personally found to be unacceptable—there were other provisions I regarded as unrealistic. In the main though, I took the view that the voluntarist case for reform was finished.

Public contempt for the disruptive effects of strikes and the strong public belief that the country's economic welfare was endangered by the high level of industrial conflict — whether right or wrong — could no longer be ignored. Ironically it was unfortunate for the unions that the 1971 Act was just before its time, and the unions had every historic justification for their suspicion of the law. In a democratic society laws need the broad acceptance of those they govern and union opposition to the Act made its continued existence improbable. With hindsight a leading union official recently argued, that given its continued existence through the past twenty plus years, the 1971 Act would have served the unions well. They would certainly have been better served by the 1971 provisions than by the laws that followed in the 80s.

I took on a number of interesting cases for the CIR under the 1971 provisions including the reports which legitimised the closed shop arrangements in Marine Transport and the closed shop in the Theatre. I travelled to six European countries to work on a major report entitled Worker Participation and Collective Bargaining in Europe, which covered the six countries. There were many other cases but the most significant of the recognition references began in a tiny factory in Woking. It brought about a national strike in the engineering industry and in its conclusion thrust me personally into an interesting confrontation with Ministers.

THE CON MECH SAGA

In the labour law history books the Con Mech case is a significant event in the short life of the National Industrial

Relations Court (NIRC). The case had a strong element of farce about it and provided a dramatic example of the way in which the 1971 Act could magnify the most insignificant dispute and turn it into a political crisis. But then, in truth, so much of English law is born out of similar small events.

The Con Mech case occurred against a background of legal action against trade unions for being in breach of various provisions of the Act they had chosen to ignore. The majority of TUC unions had determined that, in opposing the legislation, they would de-register thereby excluding themselves from any benefits and more significantly any legal immunity, which the Act might have extended to them. The majority of employers and certainly the big employers wanted no more than to get on with their business and therefore came to an understanding with their unions, skilfully avoiding the traps laid by the legislation. But individuals and individualistic small employers were not so restrained. Con Mech and its owner fell into this latter category.

The company was small, employing no more than 60; though it was a very profitable enterprise run from the top in a tough and paternalistic style. The plant had an odd production mix; on the heavy engineering side manufacturing large earth clearance and scraping edges for site levelling. On the other side of a wall of stacked oil drums a small continuous production line (staffed by women) manufactured small blades for bread slicing machines.

The heavy engineering work tended to be hard and dirty and in that middle class commuter town of Woking, the factory faced a constant recruitment problem. The Con Mech director found a solution to this problem when he heard of a mushroom farm at Chobham going out of business. By some mysterious process the farm had managed to import and employ Sicilian and Southern Italian agricultural labourers and these were recruited *en bloc* into the Con Mech factory. The arrangement, at first seems to have offered few problems for the company. The men were not of a tradition to complain. With little understanding of the English language and with an even vaguer comprehension of British conventions they were unlikely to be able to articulate any complaints. In some ways the men had been well treated by the company; many had acquired substantial mortgages in Woking through the good officers of the company and with the support of the local priest. No enforcement of overtime occurred but the factory remained open for 14 or 15 hours a day and the men were at liberty to work those hours if they chose to do so. A large mortgage probably acted as adequate encouragement without company pressure.

The whole arrangement seemed to have worked in a most satisfactory manner as far as the company was concerned until the owner took a fateful decision in the summer of 1972. He provided, at their request, a vacation job for two adult graduates, I seem to remember, from Warwick University. The two claimed to be appalled by the conditions under which the Italians seemed contentedly to labour over their 12 to 15 hour days. The students paid a quick visit to the local office of the Engineering Union (AUEW) obtaining a membership card for each worker and then announced themselves to the owner as the accredited shop stewards. He immediately threw them out of the factory. The two reported to the union and then picketed the factory with the union's blessing.

As the Italians left the factory later that night the two picketing students persuaded many not to return to work. The company then faced a real problem.

Some organisation—possibly a trade association—advised the owner of Con Mech to seek an injunction from the NIR Court and from there the case leapt into national prominence. It was at this point that we were drawn into events.

The Court, under (then) Sir John Donaldson, agreed to a restraining action against the union but on the condition that the CIR would conduct a survey to determine whether the union should be granted recognition. This prospect horrified the company owner. But in a skilfully engineered private session, in which I participated, the judge pressured the company to accept that I should move into the factory the following day. As a final retort the company director warned me that the majority of workers on the heavy engineering side spoke no English. Judge Donaldson raised his eyebrows to us. The Commission secretary and I agreed to the condition for our involvement and we then rushed back to complete the work on the questionnaires and, most of all, to find an interpreter. One of my colleagues located a Sicilian nun in the Italian hospital and, for a brief moment, I thought of the fun arriving with a nun in full flowing habit. At the last moment the Italian institute rang to confirm that they could provide a skilled interpreter; though we would not be able to meet with him until our arrival at the factory.

On a warm October morning I sat with the interpreter on a boundary wall alongside the factory. I ran through the procedure and posed the questions we needed to put to the people we intended to interview. Of all the questions a crucial one would provide the foundation for the Commission's decision. This posed the issue of whether the candidate wished to be represented by a trade union, but it was essential to emphasise that there was but one union, which at that point had no lawful status. The interpreter solemnly ran through the translation to the question and announced that it would be correct to enquire whether the worker would 'wish to be represented by the Syndicato Mafiosi'. To put the issue in that way to Italian workers seemed at least to be a little questionable. I arranged for a telephone call to the Labour Attaché in Rome and enjoined him into the discussion. He confirmed the interpreter's translation as correct. I went ahead and privately posed the question to each worker and in turn they confirmed their almost universal assent.

God only knows where those people are now—probably running their own factories or a chain of restaurants in London—but at that time they had all the characteristics of peasants. Their strong features were reminiscent of a Brueghel painting but their eyes betrayed real fear. We were gentle and friendly with them, but from their perspective these officials from government would surely begin to question how they came to be in the country. That issue was not one for me.

On my return to the Commission that evening I had a request to attend an informal late meeting across in the Department of Employment where they had maintained a close interest in the progress of the case. Already the NIR Court had sequestered £75,000 of the union's funds as a penalty for ignoring the court order to call off the Con Mech strike, which at that time had no more than a dozen workers in support. At the Department I ran through the sequence of events and outlined the results of the survey; two bargaining units but little union support amongst the women bread knife workers though solid support amongst the heavy labourers. I advised them that my report to the Commission would lead to a recommendation for union recognition rights for part of the workforce. How long, I was asked, will it take to write the reports? Looking to a report of no more than ten pages I suggested two to three days. Ministers, I was informed, would certainly welcome a much longer gestation for the Commission's findings.

The implication was clear. The union would continue to defy the law and suffer sequestration of its funds until it was crippled. An example for the rest of the TUC unions.

I wrote the first draft of the Con Mech report over the weekend and presented it to the Commission secretary and chairman on Monday. We recommended recognition for the heavy engineering workshop but with the union de-registered the report was unenforceable and the employer simply ignored its findings. The court went on to fine the union again, and this time compensated the company—despite the company's refusal to implement the Commission's recommendations.

In the final stage the union called a series of national strikes with support from some newspaper workers. By this time only five stalwarts were left on the original Con Mech picket line, whilst the court and the union battled it out at the considerable expense of the rest of the engineering industry. With the whole engineering industry in chaos the employers stepped in and dealt a crucial blow against the legal provisions. A group of major employers persuaded the court to allow them to pay the union's fine and wisely the court agreed; the union also backed away from the confrontation. The 1971 Act was virtually finished from that point.

The 1971 Act was aesthetically commendable. It had a comprehensive form, which wetted the appetites of lawyers, and it had the litigious minded pouring through its provisions in admiration.

In practical terms the Act offered much to unions and employers alike, but it was before its time and proved to be a costly mistake. The battle over the introduction of law into British industrial relations practice had to be fought; but the government made the mistake of believing that they would have the employers on their side in that battle. At that time unions and employers alike were opposed to the law's encroachment into their business.

A few years later the climate changed, employers shed their distrust of the law and enthusiastically supported the provisions introduced by another Conservative government which, in an endeavour to confine the unions, applied layers of penalties and restrictions upon them.

The law is now fully engaged in the organisation of trade unions and in the process of collective bargaining but in a generally punitive style. It would be interesting to see the reaction of trade union leaders were a government to blow the dust off the 1971 Act, polish it to suit the times and challenge the unions with that balance of rights and obligations which characterised that fateful and short-lived legislation.

Naturally during the period of its involvement with the 1971 Act the CIR had faced the public hostility of the unions. Employers for the most part were none too happy to see us around their premises either. Typically though, as George Woodcock had predicted, the public position of the unions rarely debarred 'informal' discussion with union leaders where one of our inquiries affected their interests.

In 1974, the Heath government fell in the midst of the coal strike and the incoming Labour government quickly set out to repeal the 1971 Act and abolish the CIR. Persuaded principally by Jack Jones, the government turned its attentions to the development of a conciliation and arbitration service, which had more coherence in its services and a degree more independence than had been traditionally provided by the Employment Department's conciliation officer and his staff.

At the CIR those of us who had served through the two distinct periods of its existence were sad to see it close. It had engaged a talented staff, its inquiries were thorough and its reports to the end were committed to the principle that collective bargaining is the best possible way to determine the pay and conditions of people at work. We argued the case for retention with Ministers but the government had its sights set on a new panacea for our continuing industrial relations disruption; in any case with a minority position in the House the Labour government needed the support of every trade union sponsored MP.

The closure of the CIR also ended the practical influence of the Donovan Report. When the door closed on the Gower Street office of the CIR it also closed on that liberal approach to the reform of our labour relations system.

Four **Civil Service**

The miner's strike of 1972 and 1973 during which the Conservative government fell from office has been well documented. The government took the confrontation as a challenge to its constitutional authority and the government lost. The previous miner's strike in 1972, which led to the Wilberforce inquiry, had inflated both the wages and the confidence of the miners. With OPEC restructuring Middle East oil output, the economic value of home produced coal increased and the miners were in no mood to accept government imposed restrictions on the wage negotiations.

In response to the economic crisis of 1971 and 1972, the Heath government introduced a complex pay restraint policy which sought to impose pay restrictions, at first in the public sector, and then into all areas of employment. To oversee the policy the government established both a Pay Board and a Prices Commission, which looked to assist in the regulation of both pay and price movements.

In its appointments to these boards the government needed to look to candidates with national credibility. The

Permanent Secretary asked me if I thought that Derek Robinson would respond positively if invited to join the Pay Board. I had known Derek since, during his final year at Worcester College, he had coached me through my examinations at Ruskin. I believed he would respond favourably, acting from his strong commitment to Incomes Policy. The following day the Permanent Secretary asked if I would pose the question to Derek and I did so.

Derek was appointed deputy chairman of the Board: he carried with him an international reputation as a labour market economist, he had an unrivalled grasp of payment systems and, coupled with a sparkling intelligence, he brought political sensitivity to his judgements. He had served as principal adviser to Barbara Castle during her time as Secretary of State and worked with the NBPI, but this time the politics were of a different cast. At the Board he led the work which established the criterion for the Board judgements and made a particular contribution to the Board's work on pay relativities which many economists find of lasting value.

The Board then found itself at the centre of the miner's strike. I saw Derek on a number of occasions during this period, once at Paddington Station as he made his way to the final show. The national press had picked on the fact that his father was still employed in the coal industry, and here was the son, adjudicating on the legitimacy of the miners' claim against the government position.

Derek finally had the responsibility thrust upon him, by the board chairman, to make known the Board's findings that the basis on which the government had made comparisons between the pay of miners and other groups was unsound. That statement, made during an election campaign, with industry working only three days a week, had a material effect on the outcome of the election. Edward Heath, at least, remains convinced of that fact.

So far as Derek's appointment was concerned, I only carried the message. I often wonder if, in retrospect, Derek wished that he had shot the messenger!

VISITING AMERICA

During my time at the CIR I made an interesting visit to the United States. The CIR chairman had an arrangement to visit Washington and it was thought prudent to have an official accompany him. He talked at the National Press Club and we visited various employment and labour relations organisations. At the American Federation of Labor (AFL–CIO) I had the first of many subsequent meetings with its long serving President, the redoubtable George Meany. We were some years later to be engaged together in an interesting political exercise. After Washington I went on to Chicago to visit the International Harvester plant at Melrose Park where an old United Auto Workers organiser told me stories of his days with Walter and Victor Reuther and his recollections of the political activist Wyndam Mortimer—a relative of Jim Mortimer who became the first chairman of the Advisory, Conciliation and Arbitration Service (ACAS).

Though I had visited the States on previous occasions, this particular visit simply wetted the appetite and I cannot think of a single year since 1973 when I have failed, in one capacity or another, to spend some time in North America. In 1975 I lectured on a conference at McGill in Quebec with Hugh Clegg and Bill (later Lord) McCarthy and then in 1976 Anne Armstrong the US Ambassador in London, kindly offered a month long study programme in the States. Geraldine joined in for the second two weeks of that programme, which took us from Washington right across to the West Coast with six stops and programmes of visits along the way. It was during that memorable tour that I determined to do all I could to be appointed to the Washington Embassy as its Labour Counsellor. That appointment, if achieved would provide a priceless opportunity to study, in some considerable depth, the US social structures and labour market economy.

THE LONDON BOUND COMMUTER

From the abolished CIR I had the luck to be selected as one of the few to transfer across to the new Advisory Conciliation and Arbitration Service which, alongside the abolition of the 1971 Act, the 1974 Labour Government established as the cornerstone of its labour reforms.

One immediate personal consequence of that move was that I therefore continued daily to spend some two hours each way in a tedious journey to Westminster. Following a local bus journey to Grays Station I would then take the train to Fenchurch Street and from there by tube to Westminster. The Southend line at that time held an unchallengeable position as the most strike ridden and most unreliable line in the country. The carriages were spartan and dirty and sprung for full loads, so that on late night journeys home in empty carriages we suffered every conceivable shock to the spinal system. On journeys into London we were packed together in a standing, swaying mass of sweating humanity, finding the luxury of a seat on one day in ten at the most.

For a blessed short time I found a welcome relief from this daily torture. An enterprising fellow purchased two splendid East German hydrofoil vessels to run a service along the Thames from Gravesend to Westminster Pier. The price seemed a bit high but the journey had both comfort and, depending on the light, an occasional touch of magnificence. The journey to London was swift and smooth and with the sun rising behind us we were frequently greeted by a London glistening in its reflections along the river. As we skimmed along, coffee would be served and our choice of newspaper delivered to the seat. It was a commuter service unparalleled by any other I have subsequently encountered anywhere in the world. Sadly the magic faded in a series of mishaps on numerous return journeys.

At that time the Thames still attracted a healthy commercial traffic along its length to the Royal Docks and much of it still carried conventional cargo. Naturally the tides along it carried a heavy mixture of debris which moved back and forth along the length of the river. On one occasion during an evening return home we lost a hydrofoil float thanks to a drifting plank of timber. On another return to Gravesend, we wound a length of nylon rope around one of our propeller shafts and burned it to a solid block with the friction.

On the occasion of an accident the vessel would slump into the water and continue its journey, but in the style of an old barge. On such evenings the journeys home were very long and we invariably arrived at our destination much worse for the enforced period spent in the vessel's evening bar room.

When the hydrofoil ceased its service, defeated by the river flotsam, I had no alternative but to return to the train. Watching commuters on that line one could regularly gain the impression that the whole population was gripped by a collective madness or alternatively subscribed to some grey flannel religious cult that encouraged mass suicide. Each weekday morning passengers would arrive at the station to hear the whistle of the station guard and the increasing rumble of the train's accelerating engine. A pack of commuters would sprint alongside the speeding train, open carriage doors and throw themselves into the opening.

Arriving home, whilst the returning train still sped at high, though decelerating speed, every carriage door would be thrown open and bodies would lean out in anticipation. At the crucial moment, with the train still at speed, they would leap as one from every carriage and hit the platform propelled forward at three times the speed they would normally run unaided.

On one morning trip to London I joined the fun and sprinted for the departing train. I wore a brand new pair of shoes and, leaping into the carriage, I was assisted by a helpful fellow who pulled the carriage door closed, unfortunately trapping my foot. My left shoe then fell from my foot and, I later discovered, deposited itself on the gravel alongside the track; next stop Fenchurch Street.

The other occupants in the carriage just ignored my plight and not a word passed between us. In London the rain fell heavily and along the road large puddles made progress in my wet sock a little hazardous. At the taxi rank a jolly driver welcomed me with the consoling thought that amongst the dullness of his life there was always 'one' that made his day. I had clearly been nominated to that position. 'Where do you wish to go now?' he asked. Obviously to a shoe shop; and I gave him directions to a store that I knew would stock my esoteric size. Then came the challenge. He pulled the cab over somewhere along Holborn, turned to face me and offered to split the cab fare if I were to go into the store and very seriously ask the assistant to provide a single shoe to match the one on my right foot. It seemed a fair deal to me.

Just after nine o'clock on a rainy Monday morning on the corner of Holborn and Kingsway a man wearing only one shoe entered the shoe shop, faced the assistant and solemnly requested a single shoe to match the one he was wearing. The assistant seemed a little perplexed and then patiently explained that shoes always came in pairs; (and his face betrayed his innermost thoughts—what a way to start a week).

'But', said the customer, 'are you suggesting that an unfortunate accident victim with one leg would be forced by you to purchase twice as many shoes as he needed?' The assistant nodded but his eyes furtively looked around for hidden cameras. Outside, the taxi driver grinned through the window behind the assistant and held up his thumbs.

As I left the store I realised that the assistant had at no time betrayed any curiosity as to the circumstances that had led to my problem. Maybe it was a fairly common occurrence!

A CONCILIATORY TIME

The 1974 Labour government speedily introduced a law to restore union freedoms—to some extent as they were before the 1971 Act. Then, one year later, a 1975 Act dignified

ACAS with a legal 'independence' that unions had claimed to be necessary for the effective functioning of third party intervention into collective bargaining. The Act laid down that the service could not be subject to directions of any kind by a Minister. That statute gave the service, not only the duty to reform the collective bargaining process, but a specific duty to promote it.

It seemed self-evident to me that the duty to extend collective bargaining was not a task that would fit easily on the shoulders of the old style conciliators in the Department. They were bred in the comfortable tradition of splitting the difference but the recognition decisions on collective bargaining made by a statutory body were quasi-judicial and could not be massaged into reality.

The solution to this dilemma could have been straightforward and Jack Jones seemed to be the first to articulate the case. The service should be staffed by non-civil servants drawn from all areas of employment. This would have reflected the staffing of the CIR and the successful way that both the FMCS and the NLRB in the United States traditionally organise their staff. This still leaves the chairmanship and board members to be appointed by Ministers.

The Civil Service unions were not happy at all with this proposition and demanded the opportunity to address the ACAS Board. Jack Jones as a board member asked them a simple question—are you affiliated to the TUC. They said yes, and all Jack's arguments evaporated and with it, in my view the essential independence of mind that service needed.

The ACAS workforce was not at one with the task the statute had accorded to them. I had to stump the country —address meetings of ACAS staff and lay out the procedure for conducting recognition cases. This recognition work was not a task that suited either their temperament or the role they had sought to play within their local communities. Many were long standing members of Rotary Clubs or Chambers of Commerce and here they were, being forced into a quasi-judicial role; being charged with the duty to encourage collective bargaining upon the members of the very institutions they had joined in order to establish their social credibility. It was an impossible mix. The adjudication of collective bargaining rights cannot be carried out entirely by conciliation officers. It is a question of social justice and must have its own decision making process, its own judgmental standards and its own staff.

For my part though there were other, achievable tasks in ACAS. The Royal Commission on the Press passed over to ACAS the duty to examine the collective bargaining practices in both the national and in the regional press. It was a mammoth task and with a strict deadline. The national study put us into Fleet Street for almost a year interviewing all the managers in every newspaper and, working through many nights, every shop steward.

The resulting ACAS National Press Report is a densely detailed analysis of the previously obscured processes of collective bargaining in each of the national newspapers. In fact the whole newspaper collective bargaining process was corrupt and based on long standing practices designed to apply workgroup pressure on the proprietors at their most vulnerable moment. Over many years the proprietors, principally interested in the degree to which they could use the newspaper to influence and impress government, had given in to workgroup pressure in order to bring out their editions on time. As a result the industry carried the burden of labour over manning. It worked with obsolete machinery and its management typically had to wrestle with, not one, but many convoluted payment systems that jointly carried within them the autonomous motivation to continually inflate wages.

I look back on that ACAS report to the Royal Commission with some considerable regret. The whole of the national newspaper industry possibly needed to suffer the challenge of an Eddie Shah on new technology. It may also have needed to go through the battle with Rupert Murdoch and his move of the Times to the high technology plant at Wapping.

Leaving aside the complex arguments on both sides, I do believe that the ACAS National Press Report typifies the weakness of the institution in that it could not possible face up to the harsh truth about the unacceptable nature of the labour practices in the industry. It is the fact of the matter that we lost the opportunity to describe the reality of the situation and then challenge the shop floor labour practices that were crippling the industry. The Fleet Street print unions were riddled with malpractices. The employers had handed effective management of their plant to the unions. After a year in Fleet Street we had the evidence to produce a report that might have stood a chance of initiating reform. The failure to achieve that left the reforms to be brutally pushed through by Eddie Shah and then by Rupert Murdoch.

Five Diplomatic Credentials

WASHINGTON

The opportunity to go to the Washington Embassy as labour counsellor came much quicker than I had anticipated. We departed without much time to ponder the implications but with great excitement at the prospect. Alyce came with us, but Steven departed to begin his degree course on the day we left for America. I felt terribly guilty abandoning him that way and it was upsetting to see him walking along the road with his backpack as we loaded the luggage for our departure to the airport. He subsequently spent more time in America during the first two years of his degree than he did in England.

The labour counsellor's job in Washington hadn't changed much since the first one took up his post in 1941. Professor R H Tawney went to Washington that year to assist the Ambassador, Lord Halifax, to get close to the Democratic New Deal politicians and to develop an understanding of the labour movement policies. The Foreign Secretary in 1941, Anthony Eden, had expressed his concern about the somewhat fractious division between the two arms of the American Labour Movement, the AFL and the CIO—a division which some believed to be capable of disrupting the manufacturing industry and consequently the flow of military supplies to Britain.

When Tawney arrived in Washington he had no brief for his task—nor did I. He arrived and had the burden of finding a house to rent—so did I. His role set him somewhat apart from the Foreign Office professionals—so did mine. But the United States I served in was not that of Tawney's day. When I arrived I found a country undergoing a crisis of confidence. The belief in the limitless nature of resources, in the capacity of man to solve all problems and the confident drive of individual Americans to succeed through their own endeavours, was by no means as pronounced a part of the national character as it had been 10 or 15 years before. It was, of course, still a land of immense wealth, populated by an energetic, friendly and often appealingly naive people. It still had a vigorous economy. It was a vast nation and much of it waiting for development and ready to absorb the rapidly growing population. In 1978, the year of my arrival in Washington, the nation's population grew by almost two million and the country absorbed that growth with little economic difficulty.

There were less attractive sides to American life, which it was easy for a short-term visitor to overlook. A diplomat, even one concerned with labour relations and social affairs, could remain only vaguely conscious of the darker side of the nation. During my time in America over 20,000 people each year died from criminal activity. Over 400,000 Americans were locked in prisons and over one million were on probation or parole. Rather more than one thousand convicts awaited execution.

A lot of the crime was rooted in the poverty to be seen just beyond the glittering Capitol building in Washington. Over 20% of Washington residents had incomes below the official poverty line. Over 100,000 of the city's residents qualified to receive food stamps.

In the 1980s almost 60% of all babies born to Washington DC residents were to single mothers and the infant mortality rate of 27.3 per 100 was as high as the rate for many impoverished developing nations.

Living, as practically all diplomats do, on the North West side of the city, it was easy to ignore the fact that Washington was a black town. Over 70% of the DC residents were black, but when Tawney worked there over 65% were white. As the middle class moved out they took with them their high taxable incomes and their children. The town had 78 totally black schools and 15 others with only two or three white pupils—all the schools desperately short of money. When the kids left, or more likely dropped out of the city schools there were few jobs for them. Over 65% of the city's teenagers were unemployed. In truth they found employment in the underground economy subsisting on burglary, drug selling, shoplifting and mugging.

There was, and still is, a very creditable side to the capital's education system. Seven universities exist in the town and two had a mainly black enrolment. From these institutions many determined black students have graduated to middle class occupations and an archetype middle class American lifestyle. This newly emerging generation of middle class African-Americans will as surely change the style of the American political system as they have changed the politics of the capital city.

The American trade unions had been the mainstream diet of British labour Counsellors appointed to the Washington Embassy since Tawney arrived there in 1941. American unions, never popular as mass movements, were distinctively out of favour by the late 1970s. But unions had more severe problems than their rating in public esteem. By the 1980s unemployment tended to be at its most severe in the industries where the unions had their strongest base and the American Labour Movement suffered an erosion of its power base.

The failure of the US unions to recruit new members went back beyond the 1980s unemployment. From 1970 to 1980 the United States economy grew at a rate unmatched by any modern society. Twenty one million jobs were added in those 10 years but union membership stuck at 22 million—some 21% of the labour force. This failure to ride the rise in new jobs had a complex of causes. The US labour law certainly did not help the union efforts to recruit and organise in new technology industries. The National Labor Relations Act (NLRA) excludes supervisors and anyone with managerial responsibilities from the statutory provisions covering union elections and the newer industries had a relatively high proportion of managerial and a lower proportion of manual staff. The predominating ethos in America puts a high value on individual effort and individual acquisitiveness which fits uncomfortably with the collectivist nature of union organisation

GEORGE MEANY

I had talked with George Meany the President of the AFL–CIO on two occasions prior to my arrival in Washington as a member of the diplomatic corps. Then on my first day in the Embassy I had a call from George Meany's factotum son-in-law, Ernie Lee, to ask if I would see 'Mr Meany' that day. What does he want? seemed a necessary question. He would like, said Ernie, to discuss the deal between the British government and the TUC on incomes policy. He wants to know what the unions believe they will get out of the deal.

My books and papers were still packed—I had memory only to guide me in the discussion. George had a rocking chair in the style of President Kennedy's chair. He began by recalling our previous meeting and then probed my background. I thought it wise (with an ex-New York plumber) to begin at the beginning and emphasise my construction industry experience. At that time I was still a member of the Woodworkers Union though by then it had merged with the bricklayers. As Clive Jenkins constantly pointed out I had the distinction of being the only member of the British diplomatic service holding such a union card. It proved invaluable in that meeting with George Meany and in many other subsequent encounters.

What is it, George Meany asked, that persuades the British unions to hold back their wage demands within this incomes policy deal. I ran him through the background and explained the union interest in expanding their role over management decision making, through a form of worker participation. There were other incentives and I took him through them.

When I finished he had a few extra questions—quite precise ones and clearly based on good pre-briefing. Then he thanked me for the discussion. For my part I hazarded to enquire whether he would tell me why he needed to know about the British situation. He rose from the rocking chair and with his stick waved me over to the window. The AFL–CIO building on 16th Street gives its leader a priceless overlooking view of the White House below. 'Down there', said Mr Meany, 'is a "little bastard" who has asked to see me in half an hour. He [the President of the United States] has visited your Prime Minister Callaghan —has a suit woven in the same initials, JC, and he now wants a deal with the American labour unions to curb wage inflation on the pattern of the British deal. When I see him I will now know what to say. If I ask for the same deal the British unions have achieved, the President will walk away', he said with a grin.

I was pretty horrified by this response, I had no remit to interfere in American politics but here, on my first day in Washington, I had walked into an involvement in a crucial negotiation between the President of the United States and the American Labor Movement. I was nonetheless intrigued by the bitterness of Meany's language. This after all was a Democratic President and by tradition he should have enjoyed a good measure of support from the Federation. It was a crucial weakness of Carter that he did not have that support. Less than a year before the ensuing Presidential elections I watched Carter address the delegates to the AFL–CIO Congress; but his address followed a stinging attack made on him by Meany from the same platform a few hours before.

Carter, in Meany's eye, had a fatal flaw—he was not Jack Kennedy. But even with that fault, Carter could have won the old man over by following the practice of other Democratic Presidents and calling Meany occasionally on the telephone. In a system without permanent political organisations, the AFL–CIO political action committees can provide a vital organisational structure for a Democratic candidate—so long as that candidate makes clear by his actions and words that he is not a creature of their making. Meany had demonstrated his own and the Federation's political power in 1972 when, in reaction to policy and procedure changes in the Democratic Party, he moved the AFL–CIO into a neutral position. Richard Nixon's election victory owed a great deal to that action by Meany.

Before I left him on that first day of my diplomatic career, George Meany tapped me on the shoulder and asked, 'do you know what this man (the President) has done to the American worker? He has caused a massive price rise in the staple diet of American workers. The price of Hamburgers is now beyond their reach'. It was no joke.

It was on a visit to my home in Washington that George Meany first indicated his intention to return the AFL–CIO to membership of the International Confederation of Free Trade Unions (ICFTU) and at the same time to persuade the Reagan Administration of the necessity to return to the ILO. The United States had walked out of the ILO arguing that both the United Nations, and in turn the ILO, had abused the principles of 'due process' which should have applied to a debate on the question of Israel's treatment of the Palestinians. The American Unions on a similar issue departed from the ICFTU in 1963. Though the US government felt little effect from the ILO withdrawal—by contrast the American Union Federation began to sense that it suffered an increasing isolation in its detachment from the ICFTU.

The British government line tended to be somewhat different, depending on the view of the particular department. The Foreign Office tended to float above such technical questions, but more pragmatic views from the Employment Department strongly argued in favour of assisting the movement of the Americans back into the international arena. Many British unions had firmly established links with eastern European labour federations which formed channels of annual visits to capitals in Communist countries to the east of Berlin. These boozy, cloistered trips to the havens of working class culture provided annual injections of support for dotty left wing politics in TUC conferences and more seriously within the Labour Party. The British government took the view that —whilst it might question the form and activity of the ICFTU and the ILO—any move which implied a drift towards a more isolationist America should be countered and if possible avoided. If the AFL–CIO could be persuaded to return to the ICFTU and from that the US government return to its seat in the ILO, then America would be playing its full part in the international agenda. That move might, at the same time, act to inhibit the two-way union traffic between Britain and Eastern Europe. It was my brief to encourage the Americans to move back into the international organisations.

In a meeting at the International Club, Henry Kissinger privately indicated that the American government decision to move back into full membership of the ILO would be consequential on George Meany's decision to retake the AFL–CIO place in the ICFTU. I held a number of informal meetings with George Meany and his staff on various subjects and wherever possible I raised the question of the return to the ICFTU.

George enjoyed visits to our home and whenever British union officers came to Washington we made a show of the event and invited the US labour leaders to join us. On one such visit, after the others had left, I posed the question to Meany as he sat in my rocking chair: When would the Federation rejoin the ICFTU? He grinned and replied: 'This year if the British make it possible and "sit down with us again"'. Acting on this indication I went to London to see Len Murray the TUC General Secretary. Meany was clearly in failing health and I told Murray that the AFL–CIO relations would best be repaired whilst the AFL–CIO leader still lived. The two leaders had fallen out over Meany's persistent criticism of British union delegation visits to Eastern Europe.

Len Murray agreed with my suggestion that a rapprochement with the Americans would be an improvement on the acrimony, which then existed between the Federations. Murray also agreed that a visit by British union officials to engage the American union leaders in a dialogue would be a sensible approach.

In its best tradition the TUC almost blew the whole visit by not including Murray but including Ken Gill amongst its delegates. Gill, the able intelligent and popular head of the technicians and draughtsmen's union had one major problem so far as the American unions were concerned—he was a longstanding member of the Communist Party. The whole delegation consequently met with a polite but somewhat distant response by the American union leaders: though individual British leaders were picked out for a more cordial treatment.

One effect of Gill's inclusion was that, as a group, they never got inside the AFL–CIO headquarters. George Meany had established a principle for admission to that building some years before when Georgi Malenkov visited Washington as the newly elected leader of the Soviet Union. Malenkov was there in the States to demonstrate the contrast between his (short-lived) presidency and that of Joseph Stalin and during his visit he attempted to meet people and to initiate impromptu visits. On passing the 16th Street headquarters of the AFL–CIO he asked his hosts if he could see inside—but it happened to be Sunday. An accompanying FBI agent knocked on the glass door until a janitorial guard came to investigate. 'This', said the FBI agent, 'is the President of the Soviet Union; he wishes to see inside the foyer of the building'. The janitor said that he would need to phone officials to get permission to open the door. The FBI agent interjected to advise him to go directly to Mr Meany. The message came back fairly quickly. 'Mr Meany says that no damned "Commie" will set foot in my building'. And nor did Ken Gill either.

Despite the difficulties, the visit of the British Union leaders managed to establish rather better relationships between the two federations. Some time after the visit, George Meany's condition deteriorated following a golf cart accident and I talked to Len Murray about the possibilities of a meeting between the two of them. Len agreed and he came to Washington to see the, by now bedridden, American labour leader.

About 10 PM on the evening prior to the meeting, Len Murray called to suggest that it might be appropriate for him to take a gift, but that he had omitted to bring one. He had been told that Meany had a liking for Liberty ties and asked if I could locate a shop that sold them and produce one in time for his 11 AM meeting the following day. Where in the name of wonder could I be certain of locating a Liberty tie? Geraldine suggested Saks Fifth Avenue store in Bethesda. The following morning I arrived there at 9 AM to find that it was training day and the store would not be opening until 10.30 AM. Waiting outside I waylaid a smartly dressed lady about to enter the darkened store. I explained my mission and told her of an international visitor and of Mr Meany's poor state of health. I struck lucky with my choice of candidate. She was a floor manager, a union member and a great fan of George Meany. I left the still locked shop with a Liberty tie neatly boxed and I caught Len Murray just as he left for the meeting. He assured me that the TUC would gratefully reimburse me for the cost. I took that as a joke!

On 10 January 1980, shortly after he stepped down from the AFL–CIO Presidency, the 85-year-old George Meany died. He lay 'in state' in the 16th Street building and AFL–CIO officials persuaded Geraldine and I that we were expected to call in to pay our final respects to the old warrior. As I looked down at that tough old man I recognised the tie: still unpaid for, but hopefully sealing a small knot in US/British relations.

For George Meany's funeral all the public buildings in Washington flew their flags at half-mast, including those around the Washington monument. On August 16, his birthday, the US post office issued a commemorative stamp and in 1994 another postage stamp carried his portrait. That may well have been a nation saying goodbye to the last of his kind; a union powerbroker with a strength that required even Presidents of the United States to stroke his ego. Longevity and long service have played their part in the power of AFL–CIO Presidents. When Lane Kirkland took over from Meany he became only the fourth AFL–CIO leader since 1886. In that time the United States elected into the White House 19 Presidents.

The American unions formally decided to return to the International Confederation of Free Trade Unions at their 1979 Convention which I attended a few months before Meany died. Responding to that decision, as Kissinger had predicted, the US government formally applied in 1980 for re-entry to the ILO.

IMMIGRANT LABOUR

The United States had an unparalleled period of growth in the decade from the early 1970s. The employed work-force grew by 25% in that period and in the last five years of the decade over one million women each year entered the labour force. By the 1980s almost two out of every three new jobs in the economy were being filled by women.

The American dream (the prospect of constant economic growth and individual opportunity) has always attracted masses of optimistic immigrants, and the 1970s and 80s were no exception. At that time the US Labor Department believed that between seven and twelve million illegal immigrants were resident in the country and were being joined by over a million more each year.

Until the public mood changed in the 1990s, the US government applied great tolerance and a measure of calculated inefficiency in its application of immigration policy. During the 1970s and 80s the US public accepted high immigration with either benign resignation or with manipulative support. Middle class households, including our diplomatic one, employed Phillipino girls as domestics without asking the obvious questions and small employers staffed out their workforce on the minimum wage with no questions asked.

The social security tax system itself reduced the degree of public intolerance to immigrants. Before gaining employment, a prospective worker needed to obtain a social security number so that an employer may lawfully deduct the necessary social security payments from employees' wages. This protected the employer from any charge that he has knowingly employed illegal immigrant labour. In our family experience a social security number was easily obtained. No questions were asked about nationality or status in the country. This might seem strange until the implications are fully considered. The social security number leads to the deduction of contributions from wages but does not qualify the individual for social security support. Claiming benefits on the other hand is a far more contentious process. Before any welfare is paid out, some searching questions are asked on the nationality and resident status of the individual.

In essence it probably meant that up to ten million immigrants were contributing funds to the social security system but could not benefit from it. Little wonder that middle class Americans felt little cause to campaign against immigration. Admittedly, the tone of the debate in America has shifted towards the more aggressive. As unemployment has risen the prospect of a mass movement of displaced people becomes increasingly possible and terrorism has added new anxiety. Nonetheless, by comparison with Britain, America remains remarkably tolerant towards immigrants.

During his time as Secretary of State for Labor, Professor Ray Marshall illustrated this tolerance to me with some figures on the 'apprehension of illegal workers'. He showed me how the Immigration Department's graph for 'apprehensions' always showed a leap in numbers just before Christmas. Marshall explained that the department received many more phone calls in this period warning it of places where illegal (especially Mexican) immigrants were employed. The workers were then caught and shipped back home. That is—they were shipped back home for Christmas. Marshall presumed that in the New Year, they then joined the flood of illegal immigrants coming over the border into the United States.

REPUBLICANS RETURN

In the run-up to the 1980 presidential election campaign most opinion polls put Jimmy Carter ahead of his Republican opponent Ronald Reagan. Few of my Embassy colleagues predicted, in their reports home, that the nation would soon have a Republican administration. I stood out amongst the few that did so. I knew that the unions had no faith in Carter. Only a year before the election I had listened as the President faced severe criticism from George Meany only hours before the President addressed the same audience.

For all its manifest weaknesses, the American Labour Movement still provides an essential machinery within the election process. The Political Education Committees are well organised and crucially important in the development of support for a Democratic presidential candidate.

Apart from the blow to Carter's credibility through the Iran hostage crisis, I knew that the unions had no heart for the campaign. I had observed the lack of zest in campaign headquarters. I had also detected a sombre realism running through a discussion I held with the likeable and urbane Vice President Walter Mondale. My diplomatic colleagues for their part relied too heavily on the polls, but I saw a Democratic campaign without conviction.

At the election, that lack of conviction translated itself into 75 million Americans who did not bother to vote. Carter won only six States and Reagan took 44. The Republicans also won control in the Senate.

A small number of American unions have a tradition of supporting Republican Presidents. In the 1980 election —true to form, the irascible Teddy Gleason put his east coast Longshoremen's union behind the Reagan campaign; so did the Teamsters and so did the unfortunate Air Traffic controllers. Soon after he took office, in November 1981, President Reagan issued a request to all agencies of government to 'adopt an open door policy towards organised labor'. He recalled his election promise to 'seek the advice and counsel of organised labor on public policy issues'. He then charged his Departments to 'give full consideration to organised labor's interests and concerns'.

The misguided air traffic controllers' leadership in 1981 had deluded themselves into believing that Ronald Reagan had some sympathy for their dissatisfaction with their working conditions and their pay. They found to their cost that, on the contrary, the President relished the prospect of a battle with a union willing to step outside the law and strike.

The air traffic controllers' leader, Robert Poli, whom I

knew well, had believed that he had a friendly line through into the Reagan camp. After winning approval from the Federal Aviation Authority (FAA) for a 6.5% increase in pay, together with another 4.8% awarded to all federal employees, the union members rejected the offer by a 95% margin. Poli then called a strike despite a prohibition against strikes by federal employees. The President himself warned the union against taking action and once the strike began, he gave the controllers an ultimatum to return to work or lose their jobs. Few of the strikers responded and the union believed it impossible for the airlines to operate without their members being in place to organise the air traffic control system. The Administration then dismissed the control staff who were not back at work.

The Federal Labor Relations Authority in October 1981 removed from the air traffic controllers union, PATCO, its right to represent its FAA members and the courts fined the union 4.5 million dollars. Showing no mercy to the individual workers, the President also barred the air traffic controllers from taking any other federal flight control jobs.

The PATCO leader did not consult his fellow union leaders before announcing the strike but its effect threw the rest of the US labour movement into chaos. Most unions responded by banning their officers from flying. In a country so dependent on air travel that decision led to conferences being abandoned, many of their activities being curtailed, and crucial seminars and meetings being cancelled. It led to a switch in conference venue by the Printing and Graphic Union from Hawaii to Detroit. Sadly, as it happened I had been selected by the union President, Ken Brown, as its main guest speaker and we had built a small holiday in Hawaii around that event. Instead I appeared before the union Congress in Detroit and to the loud applause of the delegates I greeted them with 'Aloha'.

The President's action against the air traffic controllers was supported in public opinion polls by a large majority and the other unions saw the complete destruction of the PATCO union as a major blow to their legitimacy. Following his action against the traffic controllers President Reagan issued his rather odd November 1981 memorandum requiring all agencies of government in framing their policies to 'consider the interests of organised labour'.

Remarkably, and thankfully, during the strike there were no major air crashes in the United States. Had there been so, the public mood may well have changed. On one occasion during the strike I had occasion to fly across from Washington to Colorado with the family. The pilot announced that passengers might wish to listen in to air traffic control on the passenger headsets. I foolishly did so and what I heard was positively frightening. At one point I heard our pilot being told that air traffic control had no time to steer us around a major electrical storm centre. We had any number of conflicting instructions at various points and I came to the firm conclusion that the only motivation of the pilot in offering his passengers this 'entertainment' must have sprung from his support for the strike. At one point I thought that we may be destined to provide the one crash that would change the public mind on the air controllers' strike.

LABOUR LAW IN TWO COUNTRIES

The British government's radical views on the place of unions in British society thrust me into a major piece of work mid-1980. The Employment Department had issued its Green Paper on Trade Union Immunities and officials were busily constructing the labour laws that were to provide the foundation for a succession of other statutes.

I was asked to produce a major paper setting out the effect, rather than the substance of American labour law. It was an interesting project, which in essence covered most of the areas of concern to the British government. I looked at the prohibition on public sector strikes, strikes within a contract, within public utilities and on railways. The paper also had something to say on the question of secondary boycotts, on the complexities of picketing, on closed shops or more accurately union shop arrangements. I also included the arrangements for union elections.

The Department let me know that the work had been 'influential' and had shaped some of the subsequent legislation. It was not for me to argue one way or the other in my report, but I did add a cautionary note in the conclusion to that substantial paper. I pointed out that there is considerable argument in the US on whether the labour law has had any substantial effect on the balance of power between unions and the employers. I quoted as example, the US public employees who have been hedged in by highly restrictive labour laws which, in many States, have denied public workers the right to organise and no legal opportunity to bargain. Despite this background, the union AFSCME was then the fastest growing union in the country. I also pointed out that whilst the picketing laws were restrictive, in some industries, unions carefully ignore the law and the employers rarely challenge them. The crucial factor for a British observer is that unrestricted picketing techniques then employed in some

British disputes, would never have been allowed by the law enforcement authorities even before the introduction of the National Labor Relations Act.

In the paper, I put forward a contentious view which may be disputable but which I still believe to be sound. I argued that the US labour law has had a minimal effect on the growth, size and behaviour of US unions. In fact, it was doubtful I argued, if any part of the statute or any particular decision of the courts had achieved significant effect. I maintained that, rather than the substance of the legislation, it was the 'concept of legitimacy' which the whole federal law bestowed on unions which strengthened them. Similarly union growth had occurred during and following Francis Perkins' period in the Labor Department through the Department's sympathetic support, rather than the supportive legislation she introduced.

This is not to argue that US labour law has been totally negative in effect. The concept of exclusive union bargaining has certainly shaped the collective bargaining system and has avoided the post-war British problem of multi-union bargaining at plant level. But even on this question, I argued that the concept of exclusivity is significant because unions were willing to accept it and was well established in many US workplaces before many unions were organised and able to challenge the single union deal.

The US at the time of my residence there was almost unique in the distinctive political stance of its labour movement. Unions ideologically and even pugnaciously defend the free enterprise system. They accept and understand the role of profit in an enterprise. They traditionally respond to redundancy by demanding a price but accepting its inevitability. American unions have never challenged management prerogatives in the manner of British unions. But despite this absence of ideological conflict at the workplace, American employers do not accept the unions for what they are and are constantly on the offensive against them. To most American employers a well-managed company requires a union free environment.

LEADERS GREAT AND SMALL

The Labour Counsellor's post in the Embassy offered an interesting opportunity to meet and debate with some legendary American union leaders. It also brought me into contact with some lesser mortals. Some of the union leaders were social revolutionaries around which major changes in American society had generated. Legendary figures tend to be either old or gone so I count it as good fortune to have met A. Philip Randolph at his Ninth Avenue apartment on a previous business trip to New York: he died the year after I arrived to work there. Randolph, the first black to lead a union, founded the Brotherhood of Sleeping Car Porters and from that base he emerged as a formidable civil rights campaigner. It was his victory in gaining recognition from the Pullman Company in 1937 that gave black American workers a national example of the rights they could win through collective bargaining. He organised the great march on Washington in 1963, which led to the watershed legislation in the 1964 Civil Rights Act. A friend in the American labour movement arranged the visit and I treasure the memory of that brief but stimulating discussion with Randolph of his life and his continuing ambitions for America's black population. He was in his 80s at that time, protected by his housekeeper Fannie Cornes and though not in good condition, full of wisdom and dignity. I have travelled through Union Station in Washington many times since and am always compelled to pause at the fine statue of Randolph that stands in the concourse.

The 1963 Civil Rights March on Washington, at which the Reverend Martin Luther King Jr. made his moving 'I have a dream' speech, is established as an historic turning point in American civil rights. Five other leaders of various black organisations came together with King to promote and organise the event. The principal promoter of the March, A. Philip Randolph, chose Bayard Rustin as the main organiser because of his long experience of non-violent campaigning. Rustin was a brilliant debater and gifted organiser though openly homosexual, a socialist and a pacifist. Those latter three characteristics did not endear him to many in the American labor and civil rights movements and Randolph had to engage in considerable persuasion to secure Rustin in the central organising role. I spent time on a number of occasions with Bayard and gained a valuable insight into the way the 1963 March was promoted and managed. He proved to be masterful at the enormous task. The efficient smoothness of the event, drawing together 500,000 individuals and families from all parts of America, and its peaceful and cheerful atmosphere owed something to the nature of its organiser. Of those Big Six, as they became known, I am privileged to have met and talked with Randolph, and with Congressman John Lewis who was only twenty three at the time and is happily still with us as I write.

I had long debates with Harry Bridges the International longshoremen's leader who organised the West Coast dockworkers. Harry had just retired when I met him, having built his union into a major bargaining organisation. He had achieved that strength against a history of niggling opposition from the AFL–CIO which had expelled the union from the federation, essentially as a punishment for Harry's left wing politics. In truth Harry loved to make outrageously radical statements. To some extent he had that old-fashioned romantic and myopic view of the Soviet Union; though he had no time for cold war politics and was never a political conspirator. Judge a man by his friends they say—and Harry always had employers, academics, wealthy businessmen and media people as his close friends.

In subsequent meetings with West Coast port employers, I liked to test them on Harry Bridges' credibility and never failed to receive their endorsement on his honesty and 'straight dealing'. That union, by American standards, had a remarkably clean record—the 'mob' played no part in its administration. Harry believed he had a mission and corruption would destroy his objective.

In contrast the longshoremen's union on the East Coast had a long history of corruption and a rogues' gallery of its officials have served time in prison. Yet by contrast that union's credentials were never challenged by the AFL–CIO leadership. I had little time for its leader Teddy Gleason, a tiresome conspirator whose main qualification seems to have been his talent for staying in office beyond his natural lifespan.

Gleason had cultured a talented, good looking and personable candidate for the future succession to the union leadership in the shape of Anthony Scotto from New York. Scotto, a Vice-President of the International Longshoremen's union, had been considered as a possibly Labor Secretary in the Carter administration. I met him in his New York local where he had established an impressive welfare and health insurance system for dockyard employees and their families. He was smart and well educated. I recall enquiring how many longshoremen there were in New York and he told me some 20,000 were on the register of whom 10,000 were in work. 'What decides who works and who does not?' I asked. He tapped his chest.

Scotto went to jail in 1979 for corruption. His conviction illustrated the manner of his union's wealth creation. The port employers claimed that for years they had been 'persuaded' to make payment of thousands of dollars into the union 'social security' accounts. In the trial the prosecution maintained that Scotto held the rank of *capo* in the Gambino branch of the New York Mafia. The guest list for his wedding certainly gave that impression. He married Marion Anastasia, the niece of Albert Anastasia the reputed Chief Executioner of Murder Incorporated. Scotto maintained his innocence throughout and served only a short time in prison. Some have claimed that his downfall resulted from Mafia over ambition in allowing him to be considered a candidate for the Labor Secretary post; a process that entailed close FBI surveillance. On his release from prison, Scotto and his wife went on to establish Fresco, a popular restaurant in New York city.

It would be wrong to give the impression that corruption and New York labour unions were one and the same thing. In contrast to Scotto I like to think of New York unions being typified by the talented and tough New Yorker Victor Gottbaum who led the New York government workers AFSCME. He could stop the working of that great city if he chose; though that was not his style. He was unquestionably a power broker and aspirants for political office knew where to call for endorsement. I believe he retired a somewhat disappointed man; his aspiration to lead the national union beaten down by the socialist Jerry Wurf who knew every trick in the book when it came to political gamesplay in the union.

Wurf sat on the AFL–CIO Executive Council and took on the traditional role of critic on Meany's stewardship of the AFL–CIO. It was a role previously played by Walter Reuther and in a small way by A. Phillip Randolph.

Like many non-conformist leaders before him, Randolph found life on the AFL–CIO Council to be somewhat unrewarding under Meany's stewardship. It is well known that in one major Convention Meany yelled at Randolph 'Who the hell appointed you as guardian of all the Negroes in America?' Typically, under Meany's connivance the AFL–CIO did not back the August 1963 civil rights march, though to their credit many constituent unions ignored Meany's attitude and joined the historic march. In his comments to me, Randolph, a gracious man, gave Meany the benefit of the doubt, arguing that it was more in Meany's style to promote civil rights legislation by arguing the case directly with President Kennedy.

I wondered about that theory when I met Cesar Chavez the founder and leader of the United Farm Workers Union. In essence these organisations that Randolph and Chavez had put together were as much civil rights movements as they were collective bargaining organisations. They might have organised themselves to promote improvements in wages and conditions of work but they had broader objectives—they were concerned to promote civil dignity for blacks and for Mexican immigrant workers.

By the time I met Chavez he had been embraced by the AFL–CIO orthodoxy but he knew where his true friends were—those who came to his assistance when he had employers and state officials against him. He told me of Walter Reuther's personal support at a crucial time in the formation of the union. By contrast Meany held Chavez at arm's length for many years. Meany, a New York plumber, probably saw the AFL–CIO as a corporate political machine to influence Congress and the White House. Unions were about wages—they were there to improve holidays and reduce hours of work. In order to achieve their primary objectives the unions needed to establish credibility within the political inner circle in Washington. They needed to place themselves in the mainstream of the American political system. Agitation to improve conditions for immigrant Mexicans, or a civil rights battle to open the job market to a black underclass, came uncomfortably close to the left wing politics that Meany so fervently disliked. In any case, on a civil rights march one could rub shoulders with all kinds of unlikely bedfellows. It was never my view of him but I was left with these thoughts about George Meany following my talks with Randolph and Chavez.

The death of Walter Reuther in a plane crash took from the American unions one of its most talented and inspirational leaders. I had a friendly relationship with his brother Victor who gave me the benefit of his long association with Walter in the turbulent history of the United Autoworkers Union (UAW).

The UAW had a violent history not only in picket line and strike confrontations; both Walter and Victor had attempts made on their lives and in Walter's case the attempt almost succeeded.

Walter Reuther brought his union and its federation, the CIO, into the alliance with the AFL in 1955. He led the UAW out of the AFL–CIO in 1968 on a complex set of issues associated with the AFL's international activities. Polarised views on the Vietnam War also played a part.

When the AFL–CIO walked out of the International Confederation of Free Trade Unions, its withdrawal took with it that part of the ICFTU which operated in South America, the Organizacion Regional Interamericana de Trabajadores (ORIT). The AFL then established three regional institutes to promote democratic trade unionism in South American, in Africa and in the Far East.

Reuther and his liberal colleagues in the UAW were far from happy with the activities of these three institutes. In particular they were suspicious of the role played by two AFL–CIO International officers Jay Lovestone and Irving Brown. Lovestone had been Secretary General of the US Communist Party from 1927–1929 but underwent a total conversion following his expulsion from the party. From that time he worked to promote the American unions as an international democratic force pitted against communist infiltration. As his close associate, Irving Brown followed Lovestone as International Secretary of AFL–CIO. Reuther and his brother Walter accused the AFL–CIO of allowing CIA money to be used to establish the institutes and to promote their activities. The Institutes have always taken a robustly anti-communist line. They seek to strengthen democratic unions and to promote unions that fit into a free enterprise system. In the case of the South American Institute (AIFLD), it is the degree to which it has trimmed its political judgement to fit into some brutal and undemocratic regimes that the main criticism of its activity has centred.

Whilst Walter Reuther had initially supported the establishment of AIFLD, he subsequently opposed the organisation when he recognised that private sector corporations would be contributing to its finances and would take leading positions on its Board. Reuther also reacted to the prospect of State Department financial support.

Since their creation in 1945, the three Institutes have been largely dependent upon a regular grant from the State Department, but have also received grants from major business corporations. The AIFLD board chairman at its inception was J.P. Grace, the petroleum shipping mogul. I talked to both Lovestone and Brown on a number of occasions and asked if, as trade union officials, they ever saw the source of funding as a difficulty. They always swept such a suggestion aside. They saw the world in black and white. With the whites they were engaged in a war against the forces of darkness. Of course they denied any involvement of the CIA in any of their activities and dismissed as irrelevant the arguments about corporate financing. This activity of theirs, they maintained, promoted democratic unions in all parts of the world. Yes, they said that process was in the interests of the United States government, but wouldn't one expect the American unions to play their full part in internationally extending the good practice enjoyed by American workers? In their view trade unions are an integral part of any democratic society; therefore the encouragement of democratically organised unions is the best means of promoting democracy in authoritarian societies.

I recall, during my time in Washington, an able and likeable officer of the South American Institute AIFLD,

Michael Hammer, who flew with a colleague from the Institute to San Salvador. Both Hammer and his colleague Mark Pearlman were tragically shot to death soon after their arrival—in the coffee shop of their hotel. They were in San Salvador to assist landless peasants obtain the titles of land they had been granted under the government's agrarian reform. Michael Hammer was buried in a civil ceremony in Washington, Mark David Pearlman received full military honours at Arlington Cemetery. In fact he may well have qualified for that honour as an ex-military officer, but at the time I thought that in death all pretence had been abandoned.

BRAZIL NUTS

It was the AIFLD which inadvertently landed me in a distinctly creepy situation during a visit to Brazil. In 1982 the Brazilian Employers Federation organised a unique conference in Rio de Janeiro. Its uniqueness lay in the invitation to union officials to play a part in the debates. The conference was seen as part of the abertura or 'opening door' policy of the then authoritarian regime.

The organisers of the conference looked to broaden the perspective of the conference by including international speakers and through the US Labor Department I had an invitation to take part. My Ambassador saw no difficulties in the way of my involvement and went through the necessary protocol—informing London, with a request that they let the Embassy in Brazil know of the arrangement.

Following the agreement on my participation the Americans asked if I wished to do anything else during my visit. I had just met, in Washington, the managing director of the Volkswagen Plant from Sao Paulo and he invited me to see the plant and to talk to the managers. I therefore made arrangements to visit Sao Paulo following the conference.

I then had a call from the AIFLD to ask if I would visit their school in Sao Paulo where a union education programme would be running during my visit. I checked with my Ambassador again and agreed to talk to the Brazilian union participants on the Sunday following the conclusion of my conference.

The proposed visit to Volkswagen had a number of attractions. I had spent some time in both the Volkswagen and the Audi factories in Germany and it would have been interesting to compare the production processes and to determine how the management practices had been shaped to suit the distinctive environment in Brazil.

My remit in the conference, alongside other international speakers, was to illustrate the nature of British labour relations and in particular to define the tolerances in our system and the boundaries of that tolerance and the penalties for breaking those boundaries. Like most international conferences it had a rather unworldly style; but at the same time we were given the distinct impression that we were breaking new ground.

On my return to the hotel room I discovered a note from the British Consul. He registered some disquiet about the invitation for me to visit the AIFLD School that weekend and concluded with a request for me to phone him. At 3 PM his office told me that he had left for the weekend but would I call the Embassy in Brasilia. A political officer there repeated the disquiet they felt at my prospective visit to speak to local union officials.

I questioned the nature of their concern and whether this wasn't all a little late in the day. He had only just seen my programme though he acknowledged that details had been provided by the FCO in London many weeks before. After a long and tedious discussion he admitted that the 'disquiet' arose simply from his assumption that my visit 'might just conceivably upset the Brazilian authorities'. He knew nothing of the AIFLD, nor was he aware that it operated with the full knowledge of the authorities. He had no information on the AIFLD School nor details on its participants.

I told him that I had no intention of disturbing any waters. I would simply be repeating what I had already said in the conference. The text of my talk had gone in advance to his Embassy and I enquired what on earth he could find in it to cause such concern. He hadn't seen my lecture.

The blunt truth was clear. Somebody in the Embassy thought it wrong to have a fellow diplomat from another Embassy working on his or her patch. The political officer hesitated. He had no reasons to give, beyond his disquiet and that didn't seem to amount to much, even in diplomatic language.

I hurried him along with the news that I had to leave to catch a plane to Sao Paulo. He asked if I would be willing to wait for him to phone back after checking with colleagues, I agreed.

It took about an hour before the phone rang and he came back with a startling new dimension. 'I have talked', he said, 'with officers from the Ministry of the Interior. They wish to register their agreement with my disquiet and advise you that it would not be in your best interests to go to Sao Paulo'.

I was stunned and furious. Here was a British diplomat seeming to threaten a colleague with the Brazilian state security police for daring to engage in discussions on his patch.

I left Brazil that night on a direct flight to Washington, against the political officer's urging to stay in Rio and 'have a good time', then to fly after the weekend to Brasilia to see him.

From subsequent correspondence between my Ambassador and London and Brasilia it became clear that nothing but sour grapes lay behind the disquiet. The stirring up of a threat from the Interior Ministry was deeply resented by people in my Embassy. Correspondence between us also showed our colleagues in Brasilia to be functionally illiterate on Brazilian labour practices and without much knowledge of people in the system. The most they could do was to indicate some brief contact with two Brasilia based union leaders.

The Brazilian people had an interesting description for the union bosses of that time. They called them *pelegos*. A *pelego* is a sheepskin blanket, which goes on a horse between the rider and the saddle on the horse. The horse is the worker; the rider the political and military establishment.[3]

When the politics of Brazil inevitably changed it was not the pelegos who moved into political power. The local unions quickly rejected those symbols of a past authoritarian society. Many of the local union leaders, ignored by my Embassy colleagues, moved up the structure and

3. Some used a more pejorative term for Brazilian union leaders, preferring to call them Baixeiro, a blanket between the saddle which gets particularly sweaty and smelly.

across into political powers. The central union activist in Sao Paulo the Interior Ministry Officers feared I might meet, did in fact take part in the programme I had intended to visit. That union activist and ex-lathe operator, Luiz Inácio Lula da Silva became President of Brazil.

WASHINGTON AND WIDER

The Washington Embassy post offered the opportunity for an interesting contact with many American business leaders. Most of them were international corporate figures. For the most part they knew Britain and Western Europe and part of the Far East as well as their own territory in the US. The global business perspective they brought to discussions provided an insight into the ways in which the US corporate decision making process actually works. They had an apparent insatiable curiosity for inside knowledge on the British political and economic system and in consequence I had an endless stream of requests to meet business leaders and to speak to business conferences. I had the duty to project British interests and managed to do so in conferences and sessions in 36 of the contiguous States of the Union.

This work with the business leaders allowed the detection of a number of potential opportunities for Britain to attract inward investment and these were fed into the Department of Trade and Industry (DTI) system. I learned from that experience of some strengths and quite a few weaknesses in our approach to inward investment opportunities. I returned to this area of work some years later with that useful experience as a guide.

On the back of a growing concern in Britain for the increasing social and economic problems of inner cities, the home departments began to demand some analysis of US inner city problems and guidance on the way American authorities were dealing with them. That work took me into some of the worst areas of Chicago—still undeveloped after the riots—into Detroit with its then frighteningly unpopulated city centre and of course into New York's Harlem.

In all of these economically and socially depressed areas I met some of the most inspirational of community leaders. For the most part they lived where they worked— in the midst of the social problem. Not for them the commute to a leafy suburb.

In Philadelphia, for example, I had the guidance of a charismatic black leader, the Rev. Leon Sullivan. He sat on the General Motors main board and had acquired an international reputation for his 'Sullivan' employment standards, which he framed for US companies operating in South Africa. His Sullivan Principles were later adapted by Kofi Annan as a Global Compact for the United Nations.

Sullivan's church in Philadelphia hummed with activity every day of the week. The building housed a gymnasium, a crèche, a youth training scheme, activity programmes for the elderly as well as all the usual church activities. He told me of his struggle to persuade black youngsters to stay on in school. He had achieved some success with a range of job compacts as inducements for those who did not drop out. He applied some courage, and achieved success too in his approach to the employment prospects for his trainees; attempting to shift cultural attitudes to open up new job areas. He described the negative views of the black youngsters faced with low grade work, waiting on tables in restaurants, as a total block on their ability to progress up the catering employment industry. So long as black youngsters reject jobs because they regard waiting on tables as service and demeaning, then they deny themselves the opportunity to be promoted to manager and eventually to own their own place. He had a novel way to approach the issue. He believed that, in part, their resistance arose from the fact that few of them had ever been out for a meal or had been served food by a waiter. The kids did not even have that elementary experience to guide them; so as the first step in their training Sullivan took them for a meal, in groups, to a local restaurant where they could observe the catering system from a consumer's view.

Sullivan established similar training programmes for minority youngsters across many States through his organisation. When I met with him he had over 30,000 enrolled in programmes. He was a remarkable man!

DIPLOMATIC IMMUNITY

Happily my mother remained fit enough to visit Washington twice during our time there. On one occasion she came to a reception at the Embassy for a group of visiting dignitaries. As always on these occasions American guests were invited to meet the visiting Brits. I retain a memory of my mother holding court on one side of the Embassy rotunda, regaling successive American guests with stories in which, I guess, I figured as the source of amusement.

Towards the end of the service in Washington I distinguished my diplomatic career by successfully claiming diplomatic immunity. That fact should not go unrecorded, for it is no mean achievement in diplomatic service on the territory of our partner in the 'Special Relationship'. I believe that I remain the only British diplomat to be granted that immunity in the US.

During our time in Washington we rented an attractive house along the road which follows upstream the Potomac River to the West of the city. The house owner had some occupation which kept him in the trouble spots of the Middle East. He seemed to spend an uncomfortable amount of time in Beirut at a time when the shells were falling on all parts of that city.

One autumn day, in response to the doorbell, I had a legal document thrust into my hand as I opened the door. It took some time to interpret the document but it eventually became clear that the Internal Revenue Service had a lien on our rental payments, in reaction to a purported underpayment of tax by our landlord. The IRS order required me to pay all future rents to the IRS until the landlord's debt had been discharged. Quite simple, except that I had a deposit on the house worth some thousands of dollars and the lease gave the landlord the right to retain the deposit in the event of any failure to make payment of rents due to him. Non-payment could also result in a termination of the tenancy, leaving us to find new accommodation with a record of non-payment as a pretty poor recommendation to any prospective landlord.

I phoned the IRS to plead my case. The IRS case against our landlord Mr D was not an issue for me—they should settle the problem directly and leave me, an innocent third party, out of it. I pleaded that it would be quite impossible for me to divert my rent to them as requested.

I had a most sympathetic hearing from the IRS official

and he agreed with my characterisation of my position as being the innocent victim. What, I asked would be the consequence of my disobeying the order. He advised against that course of action. 'We already have an order out to sequestrate funds from your personal bank account', he said, 'and if you decide to divert your money to other accounts we would simply take possession of your two cars'. Sympathy he offered in quantity but concession was not in his frame of reference.

In a phone call to Beirut I talked to Mr D but he denied owing the IRS anything and seemed disinclined to take any action to protect me. In desperation I saw the Ambassador and with one mighty diplomatic leap I was free.

The event with the IRS illustrates a less than loveable side to American society; its litigious nature which produces a good living for almost a million practising lawyers. Some economists have begun to question whether the malaise afflicting many big American corporations can, in part, be laid at the door of the long and expensive American legal process. Lester Thurrow the distinguished American economist subscribes to that view and described to me the events which illustrate his point. In the winter of 1982 a 747 coming in to land at Boston overran the runway to crash into the water. Two people were killed. A year later the relatives were suing the airline, the airline suing the airport, the airport suing the snow clearing contractor, the contractor suing the construction company which laid down the runway.

By a horrific coincidence, two days after the Boston crash, a 747 arriving into Tokyo landed in the harbour, killing a number of passengers. The day after the crash the President of the Japanese airline, JAL, personally travelled to the house of each Japanese passenger killed, to express his sorrow. One month later the airline had settled all compensation claims with the relatives of victims. I understand that the American litigation went on for almost ten years.

AMBASSADORS THREE

I have carefully avoided, in this part of the text, any discussion of the many sensitive and confidential issues I dealt with in my time in Washington. These included the negotiation of a social security agreement with the Americans and some activity to detach the American unions from their allegiance to the IRA. Similarly I break no confidences from discussions with three Ambassadors I served, though in Sir Oliver Wright's case the contact was minimal since he arrived towards the end of my time there.

I had a good working relationship with the brilliant intellectual Peter Jay and with his successor, that doyen of diplomats Sir Nicholas (Nicko) Henderson. Peter Jay was not altogether popular with either the Foreign Office diplomats nor with the British military top brass in Washington. The diplomats worried over whether his appointment might start a general trend, with the government making political appointments to ambassadorial posts in the American style. The military disliked his capacity to master their brief—in a few cases better than some of them had managed to do so for themselves.

Jay established a close relationship with Zbigniew Brzezinski the National Security Council Advisor and used that relationship to master some of the complexities of East / West relations. From that knowledgeable base he went on to question some of the assumptions underlying the views of the military advisors who gathered around his table at the Friday morning meetings. It was not a process which lent itself to success in the internal Embassy popularity stakes.

Peter Jay and Jimmy Carter also had a lot in common. They were both conceptual, as opposed to practical thinkers and Carter found Jay to be more open minded in discussion than he had experienced with professional diplomats.

Nicholas Henderson came to Washington following Ambassadorial posts in Bonn and in Paris. In Paris he had reached the traditional Foreign Office retirement age at which point he penned his confidential valedictory report. By a mysterious route, but with perfect timing, his report found its way into the pages of *The Economist*. This ensured that its contents caught the eagle eye of the new Prime Minister; she approved of its sentiments, persuaded Henderson not to retire and had him appointed to the Washington Ambassador's post.

After the Henderson's arrival, the modern art, introduced to the residence by the Jays, was crated and despatched to London to be replaced by more traditional paintings, which more comfortably filled the panel spaces throughout that grand Lutyens building. Invitations to the Ambassador's lunches and dinners, under the guidance of Lady Henderson were again keenly sought by top Washington political figures. Under her skilful eye the rose garden again flourished. The change from the young, intellectual, epigamic Jays, to the more diplomatically sophisticated Hendersons, also reflected a sharp change in Washington lifestyle.

I made my first visit to Washington during the Kennedy

administration. The District had a bubbly vitality; film stars by the hundred came to town; receptions were invariably black tie and dinner jacket, the events usually full of glitz.

My next few visits were during the Nixon era. Washington—a political chameleon of a town—at that time had for me an unavoidable air of conspiracy. The change of administration from the Democratic Jimmy Carter, to Republican Ronald Reagan also produced a change in both the acceptable standards of dress, and in the style of official receptions. With Reagan's inauguration the business community returned in force, bringing with it a distinctive social ethos.

As with Presidents, so each British Ambassador sets both the intellectual tone and the dress style for his period in office.

Ambassadors, for combined security reasons and confidentiality, tend not to dine out in restaurants. Against this general protocol I nonetheless proposed a lunch at Tiberios for Henderson and the new AFL–CIO President Lane Kirkland in order to establish a relationship. I knew that they had at least one thing in common—a taste for and an expert knowledge of good French wine.

At the lunch they jointly thrust the choice of wine upon me. The wine waiter, watching my hesitating hand moving slowly down the page, with the price increasing with each move, bent to whisper advice. With these two gentlemen you would be better somewhere near the bottom. I cannot recall the wine but I do remember the bill; for the modest quantity of wine set back my expenses for the rest of the year.

The meal at Tiberios concluded with a somewhat uncanny experience. The wine waiter returned to the table when the two guests had departed. He confided that he had served me many times before but that was 4000 miles away in London at Hostario Romano. On a trip back to London I ate there again to be greeted with the news of their ex-colleague who had written to tell them of the encounter. Sadly that lively eating house, which consistently served the best lamb in London, is now long since closed.

I served in Washington during the Falklands war with Argentina and observed Henderson's tireless and skilful involvement with the White House and State Department during the crisis. I also saw most of the telegram traffic between London and the Embassy during that period— some of the text was frankly hair-raising.

Foreign Office telegrams tend to be drafted in a distinctly cryptic style with a sprinkling (from senior level) of ironic humour. A colleague, David Thomas, achieved promotion from Washington to become Ambassador—in Cuba. Soon after his arrival an armed intruder found his way into the Havana Embassy and into the Ambassador's room where he held David Thomas at gunpoint. After some considerable time the Ambassador persuaded the man that they could both benefit from a drink and the gunman allowed David Thomas to ring his assistant with a request for refreshments. Once in the room the assistant managed to overpower the gunman. The resulting telegram from the Foreign Secretary, Lord Carrington (copied to Washington) was a classic of its kind.

AMBASSADOR THOMAS.
CONGRATULATIONS ON YOUR CHOICE OF
MANSERVANT.
CARRINGTON

In my time in Washington I observed high drama and tragedy and farce. I sat in the union convention to hear President Reagan and was there as Hinkley shot Reagan on the pavement outside. On 13 January 1982 I happened to be driving in the snow adjacent to the Potomac's 14th Street bridge, when the 737 Air Florida plane bound for Tampa from National Airport ploughed into the bridge killing all but five people in the plane and some of those driving cars over the bridge. I observed the glittering occasion of Margaret Thatcher's Embassy dinner, with President Ronald Reagan as principal guest. I spent some hours in enraptured discussion with the Democratic Speaker of the House, Thomas P (Tip) O'Neill. I had a long session with the young Reverend Jesse Jackson discussing his 'work ethic' schemes for inner city black youngsters. Just before our departure from Washington I had the opportunity to meet and talk with a man I had long admired, Justice Thurgood Marshall, the great civil rights lawyer who became the first African-American to be appointed to the Supreme Court. He wrote some of the finest dissenting opinions, many of them on the cases concerning the death penalty—to which he was implacably opposed—and on issues of discrimination.

Marshall was fairly abrupt in his responses at first but warmed when I mentioned that I had met A. Philip Randolph. Justice Marshall told me that his father had worked on the Pullman Cars. He relaxed even more when I told him that I had read his—minority—dissenting opinion in the Texas San Antonio School District Case in which he had argued that education is a fundamental constitutional right. I managed to get him to talk a little about his early experiences as a civil rights lawyer, often working in hostile environments in the South

As time drew near for our return to Britain, we began to realise how great a wrench that departure would be. We would miss our American friends and the open nature of American society. We would also miss the warmth of the summer days and rattling cicadas. Most of all we would miss Alyce who had determined to stay in America.

There were many treasured memories to take with us. Amongst them one glorious evening of an Independence Day, sitting on the steps of the Capitol building as Aaron Copland below us conducted the National Symphony Orchestra. As the percussion boomed the final chords of his *Fanfare for the Common Man* the fireworks lit the sky, the Mall and the distant Lincoln Memorial in a harmonic blaze of coloured light.

Six Home Again

The instruction to return to Britain came as quickly as the original opportunity to go to Washington had occurred. A phone call around 6.30 AM offered the top departmental job in Scotland: it was just before Christmas but I had to be in the post by the first week in January.

The process of detaching ourselves from Washington consisted of a frenetic round of goodbye sessions punctuated by bouts of selling as we disposed of our cars, electrical goods and a hoard of 'collectibles' we declined to ship home. Putting the house back in a state to ensure the return of a few thousand dollars deposit also concentrated our energies. In between times I completed my valedictory report.

As it transpired, on the very point of departure, the post in Scotland disappeared under Secretary of State Norman Tebbit's iron heel. We thereby arrived at a cold and rainy Heathrow with no job and a house abused by its last tenants to which we vowed we would never return. We moved in with generous friends at a college they ran in

Ruislip to allow time to reflect on our position and await developments.

At this point I gave serious thought to leaving the civil service possibly to return to the States. I had been through some probing meetings with American colleagues in a number of organisations in New York and in Washington. They had raised the question of my staying to take on a job with them. I had no doubt that I could find a stimulating and profitable occupation were I to take the next plane back.

Life is never that simple. Steve was still at college completing his MA and might need help and a base. Both Geraldine and I had elderly parents needing support. Our goods and chattels were in a container heading for Britain; nonetheless I came very close to buying a return ticket. Then the Secretary of State's office phoned to say that he wished to see me.

There are two Norman Tebbits. The best known one, the populist politician, wrapping himself in the union flag, sneeringly contemptuous of collectivist institutions such as the European Community, trade unions and the welfare state. Then there is the Tebbit one meets in private, employing good natured banter and jokes, a willingness to debate and to consider ideas. It was this latter Norman Tebbit with whom civil servants of most persuasions enjoyed working.

At our meeting we talked around the work I had done in America. He complimented the style and content of my reports and said that he had enjoyed reading my valedictory paper. He moved on to test out my views on the place of law in labour relations. I referred him to my report of the functioning of American labour law, which from an

American perspective covered all the main aspects of the Department's Green Paper. In my view the law had to be balanced in its construction of rights and obligations, providing for and bearing on all sides equally. Labour Law in particular needed to avoid providing lawyers with a lucrative living at the expense of employers and workers. The law also needed to provide open and equal access. To have long term credibility the law had to be acceptable to those to whom it applied. Set against these standards, I told him, the government's labour law proposals were seriously deficient. He asked for a practical example and I responded that a viable legal framework had to include provisions, which allowed unions to achieve recognition rights.

At the end of the discussion Tebbit said that he did not agree with many of my basic premises, but that had we engaged in the debate prior to his decision on Scotland then I would have been appointed to the post.

It was gracious of him to privately admit his error. But I could not resist the opportunity to say that it should be fairly easy for a Secretary of State to arrange events in just that way should they have a mind to do so.

The same day as the Tebbit discussion the Department made the offer of a number of jobs from which I chose to go initially to the Manpower Services Commission headquarters in Sheffield, and then to the Northern Regional Director's post. The job had an added responsibility to establish inner city regeneration teams to promote economic activity in the cities of Newcastle, Sunderland, Darlington and Middlesbrough.

It was an oddity of that short-term Sheffield job that a lot of the serious work had to be done in London. Where that required an overnight stay, if alone, I took to eating at Wheelers in Soho. Perched on a stool at the counter I would invariably find someone interesting to talk to over the meal.

Around the end of May 1985, I sat at the end of the counter next to a gnomish fellow wearing a leather jacket. He gave the impression that he had been drinking for some time and insisted that I join him in sharing his wine. He was similarly persuasive in ordering a joint helping of whitebait which I, at first, resisted, on the grounds that I could not stomach all those staring eyes. I gave way and we shared an enormous plate together. As we ate and drank, he enquired if I had any experience at printing and design. He had an exhibition recently opened but, in his view, the 'incompetent reproduction and shoddy layout of the catalogue', which he claimed had been undertaken by top designers and printers, threw into question the ability of anybody in Britain to produce a catalogue of first class quality. Do we have to go to Italy to get the quality all major exhibitors expect, he asked.

Having previously told him of my recent return from America, my companion enquired if I liked any American art. I mentioned a liking for Andrew Wyeth and Edward Hopper. Most of all though I admitted to enjoying Georgia O'Keefe: her work was so redolent of the desert areas of New Mexico. Her art had grown out of her environment.

My companion rejected that notion. There was every possibility, he argued, that O'Keefe had gone to that environment because it suited her art—and her arthritis!

The conversation wandered through various subjects, 'Which European city did I like best?' Did I like Australian wine (somewhat of a novelty at that time). What did I think of Spain?' But the discussion always came back to aspects of art.

He asked if I had been to any art exhibitions during my stays in London and we briefly discussed some of the art I had seen in the previous few months.

'What motivates a civil servant', he enquired. 'What motivates an artist', I responded. 'A typical civil service response', he quietly rapped back. But he told me what motivated him. It was simply for him, a process of interpreting his senses and translating that interpretation into images.

I slowly recognised my stupidity. I had been engaged for two hours in a discussion with Francis Bacon. When we parted, he paid me the compliment of saying that, though I knew little about art, I did know a lot about the way to argue a case and we should meet at Wheelers again for a drink. Sadly, soon after, Wheelers chose to 'tart up' their restaurant, losing his custom and mine.

In the, thankfully, short time I spent at the Manpower Services Commission (MSC) I had the testing experience of dealing with the decidedly oddball Minister of State, Peter Morrison. His reputed capacity for hard drinking and the alarming rumour of him being apprehended by police on suspicion of deviant behaviour had clearly stamped him 'treat with care'. Morrison added to that health warning by his practice of marching around the MSC building at 8 AM and charging into rooms to see if he could find anyone having an early morning read of *The*

Guardian—his bete noire. To his delight he once discovered some of my staff playing early morning computer games and castigated them for wasting taxpayer's money. It was a typically stupid act and I had the pleasure of telling him that the 'game' was part of a structured computer-training programme. I had to ask if he didn't think it wise to leave the management of the staff to me and for him to concentrate on policy.

The really interesting confrontation with Morrison came later when I met him at his Ministerial office in London. One small bit of work carried out in my Directorate, concerned the sponsorship of training programmes for managers in industry. Morrison asked me to run through each programme giving its objectives and the target management group. I had never thought highly of all the programmes but I did hold the view that, measured by the best international standards, British Management of the time had plenty of room for improvement. The programmes were based on the premise that well designed, accurately targeted and effectively managed training could improve performance. It was a view supported by the main employer federations.

Morrison listened as I went through the general details of each programme. As I concluded each one he said, 'Get rid of it'. He was unmoved by the fact that contracts existed with the training providers and companies had paid for managers to attend and cancellation would be very costly.

After two hours he had wiped out half the programmes. We were then interrupted by the arrival of his nephew to accompany him on a lunch appointment. That would clearly finish Morrison off for the rest of the day so

I retained some hope for a reprieve.

I returned to the office, pulled out all the background files on the programmes into a literal mountain of paper and began to work systematically through them. My instincts told me that somewhere in that mountain there existed a bit of evidence that would provide a defence against Morrison's butchery of the programmes. The idea that government money should be spent on training everybody except the managers was patently absurd. In restructuring the labour market, the whole labour force needed to be equipped with new skills. I stayed very late into the dark hours and had a neat reward for my labours. A letter in the file from Norman Lamont, then junior Minister of the DTI, argued that the relatively low productivity in British manufacturing industry could be attributed in part to the poor performance of managers. He maintained that the training agencies had failed to engage effectively in the training of managers and he called on the MSC to support a wide range of programmes.

On the basis of that letter I persuaded David Young,[4] the chairman, to request a meeting of junior ministers from the main economic departments to hear a proposition for a widening programme of management training. He promised to chair the meeting, but on the day he had to dash across to Number 10 to see the Prime Minister and that left me in the hot seat surrounded by a Ministerial team containing Morrison. I think that another lunch meeting intervened and Morrison left half way through my peroration, the rest of them gave my proposition their strong backing. Oddly, Morrison never referred to the

4. Later Lord Young of Graffham: Secretary of State for Employment and Secretary of State DTI.

issue again. His whole approach typified a capricious side to British politics that has, for generations, undermined effective governance.

Morrison held another Ministerial office before he went to serve as deputy chairman of the Conservative Party. To Margaret Thatcher's great cost she relied on his faulty intelligence gathering and unhelpful advice during the 1990 putsch that removed her from office.

LEADING THE CITY ACTION TEAM

With considerable relief I moved into the Northern Regional Director's post of what was then the Department of Employment in October 1984. The responsibilities covered the traditional range of departmental functions —administration of the Northern Job Centres, Youth and Adult Training Programmes, job inducing programmes, disabled employment and all the usual peripheral departmental responsibilities. I also took on the duty, which had attracted me to the northern post, the leadership of the City Action Team (CAT).

City Action Teams were based upon a perfectly correct assumption that economic departments of State needed, at regional level, to co-ordinate their policies, activities and spending into a single strategy if they were to succeed in contributing to the regeneration of Britain's industrial cities. It was a policy to which the government returned some ten years later when, in 1994, it established the integrated government offices in each region.

In truth the government saw the City Action Teams as excellent vehicles for projecting government policy. From the onset, the seeds of a good idea were almost swamped in a tide of glitz and public relations hype. We were launched by Ministers with glossy brochures and video presentations, but no extra money. The CATs were received with considerable cynicism. On the day after their launch, April 19th 1985, *The Guardian* capsulated this cynicism with a cartoon showing three bowler-hatted musicians, The CATs Merry Dance Band, greeting an impoverished musician in a derelict street. 'The Lady at Number 10 says she hasn't got any money to give you—but perhaps you would like some music lessons.'

In my own role I had to overcome another problem. My co-directors, Reay Atkinson and Alistair Balls could hardly be expected to welcome a newcomer to be their Team Leader. Alistair became a great support and later moved to head the Tyne & Wear Development Corporation, where he applied his immense energy to the transformation of the economic and social environment along the banks of the two rivers. Reay, for his part, remained his irascible self throughout, though he subsequently gracefully volunteered the view that I had turned a piece of government hype into real economic achievement.

I soon decided that the bulk of my department's work, other than the City Action Team, needed the addition of a colleague with different talents to mine. I had the luck to recruit an ambitious and able deputy, Ken Pascoe, who took over the main departmental responsibilities, freeing me to throw myself into the City Action Team activity.

We set about to tailor many of the departmental programmes to meet the CAT needs. Then, in a meeting with Lord Young, I convinced him that the CAT should operate in the inner cities of Sunderland (to meet the problems of shipbuilding decline) and Middlesbrough as well as the

Newcastle-Gateshead conurbation. I also persuaded him that the CAT directors should be committed to work together in all areas of the region.

We needed extra money and during a deliberately organised long car journey on one of his visits, I attempted to convince Lord Young that a small amount of extra money would produce a major effect, given our co-ordinated programmes.

We had the projects designed and ready to begin: given the seed capital to promote them we could show results within months. Within a few days I had a reply from Kenneth Clarke, then the DTI Minister, providing the requested resources. From there began a hectic and rewarding activity.

The mid-80s saw the North East of England in the midst of its worst economic decline. Coal industry closures were accelerating, the steel industry in Consett disappeared and commercial shipbuilding faced its mortal blow with the decision by the government not to provide work for or subsidize its production. I went with the Industry Minister, Tony Newton, to meet the Save Our Shipyards Committee at which he made clear the government's intention. Immediately before that meeting I took him to the Ropery, converted into a high-tech training centre. Some years before its conversion, the Ropery had produced ropes for most of the ships built on the river Wear. Bob Cooper, the owner of the company, which ran the centre, told the Minister of archaeological evidence indicating that shipbuilding on the Wear could be traced back almost 1,000 years.

Newton had few of the hard-nosed attributes of the Thatcherite politicians of the time and it would be good to believe that his long period in one public office or another owed something to his civilized behavior. He had the sensitivity and intelligence to see the decision to close the shipyards in its historical context. In effect, it was the end of a thousand years of shipbuilding on the River Wear.

Unemployment had risen, in the North East to a high of 18%, but it was also heavily concentrated into areas where few new employment opportunities existed. There were particular housing estates where virtually every household relied upon some form of state welfare benefit.

Yet in the midst of this depression there were significant signs of the economic investment, coupled with brash optimism, that gradually but positively regenerated the region's economy over the following ten years. John Hall began the construction of Europe's biggest indoor shopping mall. Before shipbuilding had finally gone from the Wear, Sunderland had been chosen as the site for Nissan's European production plant. On the back of that success, all the North East local authorities, together with the business community and trade unions, assisted by Government departments in the region, came together to form the Northern Development Company (NDC) as the instrument to continue the process of attracting inward investment.

Not that these developments were received with universal acclaim. Plenty of voices were raised against the import of Japanese 'screwdriver' jobs. John Hall's Metro-Centre would destroy the commercial centre of Newcastle: it would fail because of low earnings in the NorthEast: or it would fail to attract customers as a result of the low level of car ownership. These views were soon to be rubbished by events.

At that time negative attitudes extended widely in the

North East. One academic in the region continued for almost ten years to propound the thesis that inward investment did not increase the number of jobs in the economy and had a neutral, if not negative effect on economic growth. As the long-term impact of inward investment on the NorthEast's economy began to be apparent to even the most cynical of observers, he shifted out of both his university and his thesis.

We determined, in the City Action Team, to work within the areas of most acute deprivation. We aimed to promote job opportunities linked to training programmes: to provide facilities which encouraged small business: and by concentrating the resources of the three departments, to endeavour to achieve the greatest economic effect by attracting investment.

To drive the CAT work, I took on a team of people with Vince Robinson as their head and I drove them at a furious pace. In four years we successfully promoted hundreds of projects: none were too small and none too big. I still believe that we had a discernible impact on the attitude of business, on the policies of local authorities and certainly upon the policies and behaviour of Government departments.

Assisted by Newcastle Breweries, we started our work with the conversion of the brewery's old stables: a fine building in a street of Georgian houses which we turned into managed workshops for small businesses needing a city centre location. It was officially opened by Prince Charles. We commissioned the construction of a riverboat in an endeavour to open the Tyne to tourist traffic. We sponsored exhibitions, developed many other managed workshops and established a pattern of high quality training programmes linked into job compacts with local employers.

We achieved one of our most satisfying projects in the conversion and development of an old, semi-derelict clothing factory belonging to Hepworth's. Ralph Halpern, the then chairman of the Burton Group, donated the factory to the project and McAlpines agreed to manage the redevelopment of the factory on our behalf. In that way, we constructed the Design Works, a centre, which eventually housed companies involved in every aspect of design.

My career path crossed Margaret Thatcher's political trajectory at numerous points in my various roles. I cannot say it was ever a great pleasure; more a high risk encounter. One occasion for example I had to greet her outside the Gosforth Park Hotel for a 7 AM breakfast meeting. I told her who we had to meet her and then said something about the early start for the day. She asked what time I rose. All the way in to the hotel she lectured me on the virtues of early rising and the benefit of adding an extra hour to the day.

A number of us with a line into the political system suggested that the Prime Minister 'might care to consider' a promotional event to sell the North East to the broader business community. Margaret Thatcher liked the idea and generously agreed to use No.10 for the event. On the evening of June 6th 1988 a galaxy of the big players in British industry gathered in Downing Street together with the industrial leaders and development agency players from the North East. The PM led the event with a call for British industry to play a part in the regeneration of the North. She implied the role to be almost a moral duty, but a duty that would directly benefit shareholders as the economy improved.

The reception in the Pillared Drawing Room following the presentations provided a fascinating insight into her behaviour 'at home'. She assiduously moved from group to group pressing her case for economic action. At one point she saw that glasses in the hands of our group were empty so she nipped across the room to physically steer a drinks lady toward us. When one senior industrialist accidentally spilled his red wine she grabbed a cloth and dropped it onto the carpet to absorb the wine. At 7.45 PM a loud banging quietened the conversation. We realised that the noise came from an ashtray held in the hand of the PM. Those of you dining at the Lords with Jack Dormand should leave, as they finish serving at 8 PM, she called. 'And take care not to drive if you have taken any alcohol'. We were dismissed.

In my period as CAT Leader, we promoted over 800 regeneration projects. So successful were we, that at the end of each financial year, we had hosts of worthy projects ready to run and were able to soak up the large amounts of money from most of the other City Action Teams around the country that invariably failed to spend their allocations.

We did not change the world with our hectic activity in the CAT. On the other hand, we did generate a lot of jobs, promoted a wide range of new opportunities and put in place some helpful permanent facilities. More than all that, we demonstrated the benefits of inter-departmental co-ordination and the best way in which central and local government could work together to promote economic regeneration.

The North East economy in 1988 had begun to turn and real growth showed signs of stimulating new business. Tower cranes appeared in Newcastle and the other cities as developers regained confidence. We had an interesting experience in March of that year with a programme organised for Margaret Thatcher. She agreed to deliver the main address to the North East Businessman of the Year Awards and my colleague, Alastair Balls, organised an event at the foundation laying of the new Copthorn Hotel.

A couple of weeks before the visit we received a request to produce a first draft for her speech to the award dinner. One member of our team had considerable Westminster experience and a reputation for fine craftsmanship in speech writing. We had a session to decide the main themes and we welded together the ideas we knew the local business community would applaud, with some themes drawn from central policies of the government. Our speech writer burned the midnight oil to produce a superb address which, in the reading, we could almost hear the inflections of the Thatcher voice. It went to No. 10 and won praise.

At the award dinner, as the PM arose, I had before me the draft speech to compare her address with the text. She wandered through some old themes and then delivered another misguided homily to the business community, which they clearly resented. It was as though our speech had never existed.

The following day we gathered at the foundations of the Newcastle Copthorn Hotel to witness the sinking of a time capsule. The hotel stands on the north bank of the river overlooked by a bridge, high banking and a clear view from across the Tyne. Armed police were at every vulnerable point.

I caught our speech writer and commiserated on the waste of his effort. He dismissed the issue with the remark that in the 'long run' it made no difference. When I pressed the issue, he pointed to the time capsule as it descended into the void and whispered, 'it's my speech they will find four hundred years from now'. So is history written.

Inevitably and properly, central government looked to move the focus of its activity to the substantial task of redeveloping the old and derelict industrial areas through the creation of the industrial development corporations. With that shift in focus, the buzz would go out of the City Action Team and I therefore decided to retire from the civil service. At that point I had notice of the award of a CBE. My immediate response was to quote Jack Benny, 'I really don't deserve this—but I have arthritis and I don't deserve that either'.

Seven The Firing Line

Seven

The Firing Line

A MOVE TO THE NATIONAL HEALTH SERVICE

As I prepared to depart from my job as Regional Director in the now-defunct Department of Employment, I received a call from Sir Bernard Tomlinson, the Regional Health Authority chairman. He told me of his decision to retire and said that my name had been given as one possible candidate to replace him. He had started his search at an early date, not intending to leave for some months.

Subsequently I learned that my candidature had been favourably received by the Secretary of State for Health, at that time my old boss, Kenneth Clarke, but it would need approval from the Prime Minister. In the event, my appointment to the chairmanship was approved by Number 10 in July 1990, almost one year from the original meeting with Tomlinson.

I never had any illusions or romantic notions about the effectiveness of the old-style, unreformed National Health Service. It was full of dedicated people but it was under resourced, under capitalised and unresponsive to modern management systems. It was a service that had dispensed with my father and his heart fibrillation problems when a pacemaker could have unquestionably given him many years of reasonably active life. Its treatment of my mother in her old age was little better. Years later when Geraldine suffered repeated heart blocks the three doctors treating her stubbornly refused to accept the evidence before their eyes and came near to killing her by neglect. The service has always been chronically short of money and the patriarchal dominance of some senior consultants has made effective management of scarce resources an almost impossible task.

Added to all that, the Byzantine administrative structures offered every excuse for avoiding decisions until the crisis provided copy for the press and then promoted some reactive action. The Northern region of the NHS had 28,000 employees within the system, 14 District Health Authorities and nine Family Health Service Authorities. Below the region, it was difficult to find any ownership of the problems as they arose. At a hospital unit level, it was a general practice to blame all difficulties upon the way the Regional Health Authority distributed its resources. If a major resource problem arose in a hospital and the local press highlighted the problem, then the District General Manager would descend upon the unit; take charge and attempt to manage the problem. If the national press picked up the issue, then the General Manager of the Regional Health Authority (RHA) in turn would move in and take charge. Consequently, the system reinforced the lack of ownership of problems all down the line.

Under the 14 oligarchic Regional Authorities, the National Health Service relied upon effective management of its resources being discharged at the RHA level.

The hospitals and District Authorities resented the authority of the RHAs but were, for the most part, ill-equipped to exercise effective control themselves. Many of them were too committed to the practice of conspiratorially squeezing extra resources by ensuring that their monies ran out for the most vulnerable and news-worthy of patients at a set time each year.

Where the RHAs had the benefit of good management and sound strategic leadership the system worked reasonably well. Where the RHAs lacked effective control the system resulted in an abuse of responsibilities, a massive waste of resources, wide-spread misuse of rules to the benefit of some less than scrupulous senior managers, and an over-manning of the RHA structures to an extraordinary degree. One RHA had almost 2,000 staff with 50 in its legal department alone.

Well managed, the RHAs were capable of introducing considerable innovation. Their demise—largely by their own hand—may have removed some capability in the service to respond to the ever-increasing and constantly changing demands made upon it. In the place of the RHAs the Conservative government imposed a civil service bureaucracy.

For all their weaknesses, the government nonetheless relied upon the RHAs to implement the NHS reforms. It was from the RHAs that the statutory and practical processes in devolving trust status to all the units was driven. It was the RHAs that effectively merged the District Health Authorities together and then consolidated their managements with the Family Health Service Authorities. It was the RHAs that were used to inject financial discipline into the system. Without that powerful regional instrument and the degree of autonomy that came with it, no government could have driven through the major changes in the National Health Service within those four short years.

A CONTRACTUAL QUIRK

I took on the RHA chairman's responsibilities in August, but for the most of that month we were away on holiday. Effectively then, my involvement began in September with a fairly large number of responsibilities passed on from the previous chairman. Amongst these were a number of contracts in their final state, but awaiting the chairman's signature. One of the contracts formed an agreement with a firm of architects, Fletcher Joseph, under which that company would take over both the work and the staff employed in the RHA's Architecture Department. The substance of the contract had been debated and approved by the RHA before my time on the Board. It promised that the company, Fletcher Joseph, would receive from the RHA some three years of work in order to secure that period of employment for the employees transferred to it.

The agreement had taken over a year to complete and had gone through numerous RHA discussions and legal scrutiny. It seemed to me, that at that final stage, it would be disruptive for an incoming chairman to repeat the debate on the principles underlying the agreement. I therefore confined my questions to those concerned with protocol. I enquired if the agreement had gone through all the necessary procedures in the RHA. I asked if the Department of Health had been informed and whether the contract met the policy direction of the Department of Health. I finally asked if the RHA lawyers had approved the detail in the contract. The chief executive and the other directors assured me that the answers to all the questions were affirmative. I recall particularly questioning an oddly worded clause at the end of the contract, but was assured that it was fairly standard practice.

So, in my first effective week as the chairman, I signed that contract with Fletcher Joseph. The employees and the work then transferred to the company and for almost three years the work proceeded satisfactorily, except that the RHA role in capital allocation during that time began to diminish as the newly-established Trusts steadily took over responsibility for their own capital development. Over three and a half years later, I gave a buffet reception for all RHA staff to say goodbye as I departed from the chairmanship. On that day, a writ was delivered on behalf of Fletcher Joseph against the RHA. The writ also named me as a party claiming that the oddly worded clause in the contract provided a personal liability.

The District Auditor had declared the Fletcher Joseph contract *ultra vires* on the grounds that the RHA should not have guaranteed any work to the company, but should simply have dealt with Fletcher Joseph where that company could win contracts by competitive tender. It was a confused and inconsistent finding with some odd reasoning but it had the effect of stopping payment to Fletcher Joseph, even for the work they had completed satisfactorily.

In July of 1994 we returned from holiday in Italy to find a High Court summary judgement for damages had been gained against me personally by the legal firm acting for Fletcher Joseph—obtained without notice to me or to our legal representatives.

It was around that time that I had received, from a prestigious legal firm, an invitation, in my recently appointed capacity as chairman of the Occupational Pensions Board, to be principal speaker at a lavish opening of their smart new city office in London. Amazingly it was the same legal firm that had pursued the oddball personal case against me on behalf of Fletcher Joseph and had obtained the summary judgement in the court. Of course, I was delighted to be invited to the event knowing, that as I began to speak, at least one of their lawyers would slowly recognise to his horror that he was suing his own company's principal guest. As I spoke, I saw one man, before me, look startled as I mentioned, in passing, my interesting time as chairman of the Northern Regional Health Authority. Red-faced, he shuffled sideways out of my view as I spoke.

The personal case against me of course went nowhere. Fletcher Joseph sacked the legal firm and transferred the case elsewhere. My costs were paid, in part, by Fletcher Joseph and the RHA. The case had a number of crucial lessons—never sign anything as a part-time chairman. That responsibility rests with the chief executive. The chairman is there to lead policy and strategy.

For government the case, as with so many others, had a salutary lesson. If major changes in the institutions, in processes and in functions are initiated by government, then the audit service has to be enjoined in that cultural development and must change at the same pace. Final lesson—never rely upon your predecessor—no matter how eminent—to have done the work: re-do it yourself.

The RHA chairman's job had joy as well as pain. I had a brilliant team of people working with me. Our budgets were large—over £1.5 billion covering over 26,000 NHS staff in the region. At that time, the RHAs had a great deal of freedom to initiate health programmes, develop new practice, and commission capital development. When I took on the job a knowledgeable friend of long standing, Jean Robinson from Oxford, suggested that I should study Professor Peter Townsend's 1986 research paper[5] on inequalities of health and economic deprivation in the North East. Townsend had been commissioned by the RHA to undertake his research, but the results were not to the taste of Ministers at the time.

Underpinned by that reading of the Townsend work, together with the gradual recognition that the NHS as a whole was a largely reactive system, I developed a whole series of concepts and began to work them into applicable projects. In the first place I determined to put in place a Strategy for Public Health in the region. I intended the strategy to be aimed to encompass all the standards set by the Department of Health, but to target a whole series of regional health problems. We drew in the ideas and support of districts and enjoined medical staff and in 1992 launched our programme. It was not an easy set of options: it aimed to set firm health priorities and would have entailed hard choices. In every round of the budget allocations and planning meetings with Districts and FHSA's, the strategy would be used as a framework for the measures of performance.

5. *Inequalities in Health in the Northern Region*, published by the Northern Regional Health Authority and Bristol University, 1986.

It was a failure of my persuasive skills that, though the Secretary of State came to launch our strategy, the Department never accepted the process to apply in general. They were too set on imposing central Departmental control and setting their own Westminster-nurtured priorities.

But other initiatives enjoyed more success. The rapid introduction of the Health Service reforms inevitably disrupted the organisational structures and removed the traditional security of managers in the system. In that insecure environment individuals have a right to considerate and fair treatment. The vast majority, shaken out of their jobs by merging authorities were found other jobs in the system. Others were professionally assisted in finding employment outside the NHS.

Whilst I had a great deal of respect for the capabilities of the NHS managers, I did find to my cost that a cabal of senior managers in posts throughout the region were determined to disrupt any attempt to reform the organisational structures. They had the confidence of men, for they were all male, who knew that they had an armoury of dirty tricks to employ against anyone who challenged them.

Just before the 1992 general election I had the dubious pleasure of featuring in the main editorials of the National Health Service Journal in three separate editions. The articles were supported by anonymous phone calls from a small group of staff. Right on the edge of the general election, I called a badly timed conference of all senior managers throughout the region to set out the proposals for the structural changes. We gave an assurance that all of them would remain employed, but most would need to accept a different portfolio of work.

By coincidence I went to see the Secretary of State,

William Waldegrave, some three days later on a totally different issue. He told me that a telephone caller to the Daily Express had maintained that I had put in place a process for lifting out managers who supported the government in order to put in place a cadre of Labour Party activists. I told him what we were doing and Waldegrave telephoned the Express editor who killed off the story.

As I have gone through life I have found difficulty with the concept of a divine maker. At times though, there have been some pretty bizarre 'rocks' thrown at me that might persuasively argue for the existence of the Devil. Surely it took a Mephistophelean sense of humour to attempt, over eleven years later in 2003, to impose upon me as auditor, one of the main protagonists in this struggle?

The dogged opposition of the managers to the organizational and financial system reforms pointed to the need for a wider recruitment of managers. We considered ways in which we might provide opportunities for a much wider range of NHS staff to step across their own specialist occupations into the key general management posts. To engineer this ambition we sponsored a Health Service MBA programme at Durham University which had an open recruitment for nurses, senior medical consultants, ambulance staff and all others in the NHS who previously had faced difficulty in their ambition to move across into general management. With a recruitment of around 50 students each year from the northern region of the NHS, the programme soon began to provide a forceful challenge for every post advertised. It brought into the general management of the service an academically well qualified staff that had also experienced life as a managed member of the NHS.

From the Townsend report, I also distilled the idea of a capitation policy, which respected the existence of acute economic and social deprivation in the region. The closure of the NorthEast coalfields (from 150 pits in the 1950s in Durham alone down to none by the 1990s) left small, isolated and poverty-stricken communities throughout the northern region. Shipyard closures created a similar pattern of deprivation in the urban areas along the rivers Tyne and Wear. In some communities, patterns of ill health mirrored those of the Third World. Yet, some Ministers continued to imply the obscene proposition that the conditions in which the people found themselves were as much the fault of the individuals, as it was of the government that had accelerated the industrial decline, or the socio-economic conditions that had trapped them in deprived communities.

No matter how effective, a health service cannot cure economic and social deprivation; but an equitable service should respond effectively to it. I had visited most of these communities as part of my CAT responsibilities and I now revisited most of them to look at the health provision. Before too long I determined that we needed urgently to move resources into these communities in response to the appallingly poor conditions. We also needed to co-ordinate with the other task forces established to tackle employment and crime.

A talented member of the RHA management staff, Dr Bill Kirkup (an ex-obstetrician), worked over many months to produce a capitation policy with deprivation as a factor and we ran it through the RHA and the NHS Executive. It did not find favour with Ministers who came under great pressure from rural, therefore Conservative,

MPs to prohibit the introduction. These MPs feared that any deprivation factor would draw resources out of rural areas in order to provide for the urban (therefore Labour) constituencies. I argued the capitation policy through meetings with two different Secretaries of State. One called it 'ideologically impure'. I treated the remark as a joke and we went on to implement the policy. The deprivation factor translated into comparatively small amounts of money aimed at the most needy casualties in the system. The rural MPs though were unconcerned with need.

TAKING ADVANTAGE

Under the financial arrangements of the time, the London regions of the health service regularly ran into chronic financial difficulty around the end of each calendar year. To alleviate these difficulties, the London regions took to borrowing from other regions. With inevitable delays in construction contracts we had resources in the RHA's capital account which we loaned out to London to good effect. Over a short period we made over £6 million profit which we put to good use. I had, as chief executive, a brilliant young medic, Professor Liam Donaldson, appointed by me following the sudden departure of his predecessor. Liam later went on to be the government's Chief Medical Officer and many rate him the best CMO for generations. He has a superb mind, tremendous store of energy and very good judgement. We worked well together, began to re-shape the system and saw real changes in patient care coming through. Liam put forward a convincing case for establishing a number of research chairs in medicine; each dedicated to an aspect of medicine associated with economic and social deprivation. It was not an easy task to get the proposal through the RHA but we did so. We offered the University Medical School in Newcastle the finance to establish five such chairs. We specified that though established in the Medical School, the clinical work should be based in one of five nominated hospitals which catered for some of the areas of deprivation.

Within two or so years, we put in place three major initiatives that would in the long term alter the way the health service in the North responded to the needs of the most vulnerable and disadvantaged. There were other projects we conceived and saw through. Following a short visit to Germany, we offered—for competitive bidding—the finance to establish a modern cataract clinic run as a day surgery unit. The techniques used allow cataracts to be removed at an early stage in their development, and following the operation patients are back home within a few hours. This contrasted with much of the, then, traditional treatment which often required the cataract to form a certain thickness before its removal; a delay which, in some cases, condemned the individual to increasing blindness before the cataract removal.

I had the responsibility to see through, in the region, the organisational and procedural changes promoted by the health service reforms. When I took on the chairmanship, there were no Trust hospitals. When I departed from the chairmanship, all forty units in the region held Trust status.

The task of merging the District Health Authorities had enormous personnel problems and a statutory process, which had to go through a laborious consultative procedure. Whilst I had many doubts about aspects of the reforms, I felt then, as I do now, that the functional division between the commissioning of health care and its delivery is crucial. In the old style NHS, the DHA both funded the service and had responsibilities for managing the service delivery. The two distinct roles became confused in the process. The confusion led to priorities being debated and determined mainly in crisis: the glitzy aspects of medicine receiving the prizes and the less newsworthy, like mental health, receiving too little.

It seemed to me then, as now, that the preservation and growth of a service dedicated to the concept of universal and largely free treatment at the point of need, required a more disciplined and more responsive system of delivery.

Whilst I supported the separation of purchasing from the actual service delivery, I parted company from some of the more extreme ideologues who had accumulated in the Department of Health during the formative stages of the debate on the reforms. In particular I repeatedly challenged the logic underlying their concept of a 'market' in public health. One vital component in any effective market is an element of over supply. It is over supply which allows effective choice. But at the same time as these unworldly apparatchiks were proselytising the virtues of a market; they were insisting that in order to save money, every region should be cutting out what they regarded as the surplus capacity. Closures of hospitals began in every region, and in remaining units, radical rationalisations were introduced in clinical provision. All of that rationalisation may have made sound financial sense to the Treasury but it had no relevance to the establishment of an effective market, or to the effective provision of health care for the patient.

In any case, outside London in a wide range of clinical

treatment, the concept of a market underpinned by choice was a sick joke. How could there be a choice for the mentally ill. Anyone suffering a severe heart attack for 30 miles around Newcastle would go to the Freeman Hospital. There could be no market in cancer care.

The Conservative government, having put through the organisational changes, never did declare where the logic of their reforms would take the service. The State need not own hospitals in order to set priorities or set standards or to control delivery. The logic of the reforms would argue that, as in Germany, control should be exercised by the purchasing authorities. The logical direction of the reforms was for the Trusts to finally step out of the state sector into charitable or some form of independent status. Private hospitals could then also be drawn into the sector. The defining concept of the National Health Service is the provision of care, freely given, when needed: not the ownership of the bricks and mortar. That concept of universal care needs to be held onto carefully and diligently. In my view it is in no way undermined by moving the ownership of the capital and the employment of the labour out of the direct control of the state. So long as the state governs the provision of the monies, which are used to supply that care, then the State will dictate the provision. By moving the ownership of hospitals out of the state's control, the process would allow private developers and independent charitable trusts to replace the state capital with private capital developments that would then attract the provision of care commissioned and paid for by the state. This was the logical conclusion of the Conservative government reforms which they never had the courage to admit.

Just before the general election of 1992, the Secretary of State met with us and asked the regional chairmen to do what they could to reduce waiting lists. It was not my role to play political games, but as the Secretary of State was willing to provide extra monies, then sick patients could be treated. We moved into the task with a will. Many patients went to a private hospital and I took the opportunity to visit some of them. They did not distinguish their treatment from the National Health Service provision. The NHS paid; therefore as patients, in their own minds they had been treated under the National Health Service. It was a message the government failed to absorb.

SECRETARIES OF STATE

In my—just short of—four years in the chairmanship of the Regional Health Authority, I served under three Secretaries of State. The first, Kenneth Clarke, was a man to all the regional chairmen's taste. He is an intellectually sharp, combative and robust politician from the radical centre ground of politics. At the same time, he was also friendly and full of good humour. His successor, the cerebral William Waldegrave, gave the impression of an academic detachment from the consequences of his political actions. He was, in many ways, too politically sensitive for the roughhouse character of British party politics.

Following the 1992 election, the Prime Minister, John Major, sought to redress his original error in leaving women out of his Cabinet, by appointing Virginia Bottomley as Health Secretary. She had laboured at the junior post for some years, but few rated her chances of a Cabinet post. She came to the position with a personal self-assurance belied by her fragile grasp of the issues. With her elegant figure and handsome face she combined a smooth delivery of prepared briefs, absorbed for the occasion, riddled through with numbers and quoted as gospel. None of it convinced and she found little public favour.

In our regular dinners with her at the Stakis St Ermins Hotel in London, the regional chairmen were treated to a mixture of schoolmarmery and coquetry. As an irreverent junior Minister whispered to me during one evening dinner 'a politician of the dominatrix school'. In reality, she had neither the political acumen nor the required physical attributes to become anywhere near proficient at either.

Prior to her elevation, Bottomley had drawn on her social worker background to specialise in social care as a junior Minister. She had taken responsibility during the Thatcher government for promoting the Care in the Community programme. As Secretary of State she conveyed insecurity in practically every other policy area but that one.

The case for moving away from very large institutional care facilities in mental provision was and still is unarguable. Even in the second millennium too many still exist. But if those large institutions are taken out of service then new provisions need to be commissioned well before, in some cases years before the old institutions are closed. To effect a humane and patient sensitive transfer, a whole range of alternative provisions need to be planned and commissioned. That requires capital funding, planning, co-ordination with local authorities and other agencies.

Bottomley promoted Care in the Community as a 'liberal' policy. She talked glibly of providing choice for patients. At the same time she constantly talked of the need for bed reductions and cost savings. When it was pointed out to her that choice requires excess capacity, she dismissed the point as an irrelevance.

There is a demonstrable case for treating mental health patients in community based facilities. Where appropriate they can receive care at home. But in the view of many informed people in the service, the programme virtually abandoned many thousands who were suffering from varying degrees of mental illness or personality disorder, as they were discharged from or were refused institutional care. Large numbers were destined for the streets, with occasional night shelters the most they could expect. A large proportion of them had difficulty coping with the welfare systems, with social services and with any kind of employment.

An insignificant extra resource went into the social service budgets of local authorities, to help them deal with the effects of the discharge of patients. Practically no new capital developments were put in place to provide alternative assisted care. The social care agencies were swamped by the numbers they needed to help.

As the Ministerial car took her through London to the Department, not even Virginia Bottomley could have failed to see the results of her work as the shop doorways filled with sleepers.

Ministers decided in 1993 that they would abolish the Regional Health Authorities—a process that would require legislation. Before they had that legislative right, they determined that the 14 regions should be merged into eight nonsensical, geographical blocks. In our case it meant a merger with Yorkshire. A close friend with connections into the Yorkshire Conservative Party told me that the party hierarchy would mount a strong internal campaign to get their man into the merged chairman's job. The North East is not well endowed with Conservative MPs and I had alienated the Cumbrian Conservative MPs with my capitation policy. That left Neville Trotter, then Tynemouth MP, as my only, but nonetheless strongly supportive Conservative. To his credit, the then chief executive of the Health Service argued strongly in favour of my appointment but political reality dictated my departure.

On a car journey to the hospital in Middlesbrough with the Secretary of State beside me, the car phone rang and the driver said that it was a call for me from the Permanent Secretary, Graham Hart. He asked for an urgent meeting. I knew immediately that I would not be the chairman of the merged Authority. I turned to the Secretary of State and said as much to her. 'How do you conclude that', she asked. 'Well', I replied, 'If it were good news, you would tell me right now on this journey. But bad news is dirty work for others to do'. She squirmed, looked distinctly uncomfortable, but said nothing for the remainder of the journey.

Happily she was not to be the last Secretary of State I had the pleasure of serving in the NHS.

IN CONCLUSION

Before I departed from the Regional Health Authority, Peter Lilley, then Secretary of State for Social Security, sent for me and asked if I would agree to chair the Occupational Pensions Board. I have the feeling that the two Permanent Secretaries, Health and Social Security, must have met in the toilets in Richmond House and my name being mentioned. I warned Peter Lilley that I had little experience in the complex field of pension arrangements, but he seems undeterred. This was the period following the Robert Maxwell debacle and the subsequent Goode report. It became apparent that the job required strengths in systems management to see through, as Lilley described it, 'the seamless transition' to a Pensions Act and a new regulative authority. This offered a totally new challenge in the national supervision of occupational pensions.

There were other responsibilities running concurrently. I chaired the County Durham Development Company through ten years of its contribution to the economic development of that County. I chaired a socially owned waste management company from its small inception through growth to being a major regional organization. Some of my time and energy went into the film and television industries through the Northern Screen Commission, which I set up and chaired until its merger with other media organisations.

The health service drew me back as a chairman, not once but twice, and as always the health service work was compelling. In that capacity I had the experience of working to a talented and determined Secretary of State who drove through major, patient-centred, reforms and underpinned them with an unprecedented increase in resources.

At one point in time I held five chairmanships and that esoteric function seemed to have become my latter day profession. From the time I went to college as an adult student, my whole working life, including the posts held since retirement, have been in public service. I believe that to have resulted from a simple accident of history. My pre college experience leads me to the view that the management skills I employed across all the public sector posts, could just as effectively have served me in private sector employment.

Looking back at the passions and emotions underlying the events and activities set out in these pages—the achievements may have been small but the process has been fun.

I now remain as restless and unsettled as ever I was in my teens and still in search of the next challenge. I am unsettled also in place and have that constant longing to be elsewhere.

I fear it will ever remain so.

postscript

A close colleague who claims to know me as a man of strong convictions, after reading the foregoing script, commented on the absence of a clarification of the author's values and beliefs. The purpose of the writing has been to provide a perspective on my involvement in events and activities for the enlightenment of another generation. My colleague argues that a clear understanding of that involvement requires an explanation of the motivating values.

One thing should be clear from any reading of the text. I am neither philosopher nor politician. In writing of these various activities I have felt an empathy with that distinguished lawyer Oliver Wendel Holmes. When similarly challenged he replied that his values had 'surely emerged from the corpus of my dissenting judgements'. In my case, the values and beliefs should be apparent from the decisions I made in the variety of circumstances I describe in the text.

When I reread this short autobiographical note, I see what I believe to be a set of fairly consistent beliefs running as a warp and weft throughout the whole account. For example I have an instinctive distrust of the authority of the State. It is admittedly ironic that a servant of the State should question the power of the institutions that gave him employment for such a large part of his working life.

Douglas Jay, my ex Ambassador's father, when in Ministerial office, famously said 'the man in Whitehall knows best'. Too often, when it comes to the interests of the majority of citizens, the opposite proves to be the case. Practically all the colleagues I have worked with in public service have been dedicated and socially conscious. Most politicians in government have been sensitive to the public interest. The insensitivity arises, not from the nature of the individuals, but from the institutional framework that dictates the decisions. The defensive nature of the government process produces an authoritarian tendency and in a democratic system the popular, and therefore the majority interests, tend to have primacy.

It is the pluralist nature of democratic societies that counteracts the authoritarian nature of the State. Single issue political organisations, robust trade unions and employer organisations, a free and vigorous press, an effectively balanced bicameral legislature, well organised local government and a politically educated population are vital components of that pluralism. In Britain, the essential components are sadly deficient.

It should be apparent from most of my work activity that I have maintained a concern for the disadvantaged. I sought, in applying employment law to enable people to overcome their economic disadvantage. In the Regional Health Service I struggled to apply a deprivation factor in the allocation of funding. In the earlier period of my working life I gave support to the process of collective bargaining that could bring a dignity to the working lives of the disadvantaged.

Support for collective bargaining rights has never encouraged me to extend any personal support to those union leaders who continue to bring to their roles the class war rhetoric of the 1930's. My father and mother treated Royalty as an archaic joke. Equally they rejected the arguments of the hard left. Instinctively they were democratic socialists. It was a natural step for me therefore to take to the 'revisionist' concepts of Evan Durbin in his brilliant *Politics of Democratic Socialism*. Tony Crosland took me further down that road with *The Future of Socialism* in which he argued that the ownership of industry is an irrelevance to socialism and that the ownership issue simply confuses means with ends. That 1956 Crosland argument echoed down the years to 2003 when a New Labour government established the case for private providers in its reform of the last of the Nationalised Industries—the Health Service. In reality the National Health Service is a concept; namely the treatment of all, free at the point of need. Ownership of the buildings and the employment of staff are a means but not necessarily related to the desired end. It is a concept that comfortably fits my Durban/Crosland-nurtured values.

In my early years I attended the Methodist Chapel, then the Church of England with the mid week activity of the Scouts. Winter Sundays were miserable days for kids in that mining town and in the absence of anything else to do, church attendance at least offered a community. The Unitarians hit on the unprecedented idea of a cinema show following their service. I became an immediate convert.

Though I have unquestionably absorbed a large measure of Judeo Christian ethics I have failed to develop a sense of the metaphysical. I have never understood why the possession of a much better developed brain than the rest of the animal kingdom, should qualify us to be candidates for everlasting life. Nor can I understand how we are expected to believe that our biologically dependent personality could survive. I can understand the need for religious belief and there have been times when I would have welcomed the ability to hold one; but that was simply grasping for an emotional prop.

This is not to ignore the spiritual dimension to life. There is something more profound than technique in Mozart, more than words in a speech by Martin Luther King, more than the interplay of human emotion in a Shakespeare play. As Beatrice Webb so elegantly expressed it—'A community of the soul with some righteousness felt to be outside itself—persisting aspirations—a faith, hope and devotion to a wholly disinterested purpose'.

I can sign up to that.

Index

Bibliography

ACKNOWLEDGEMENTS AND REFERENCES

The following publications have been either quoted in the forgoing pages, used to verify facts or, as in the case of the CIR reports, they centre on described events. I cannot avoid responsibility for the analysis and conclusions in the listed CIR and ACAS reports.

BAMBER, Greg J. and Russell D. LANSBURY, eds. *International and Comparative Employment Relations.* Sage, 1998

BRANCH, Taylor, *Parting of the Waters. America in the King Years.* Simon & Schuster, 1988

CARR, Steve, *Changing Patterns of Work.* WEA pamphlet, 1984

CROSLAND, Tony, *The Future of Socialism.* London, 1956

DUNLOP, John T., *Industrial Relations Systems.* Holt-Dryden, 1958

DURBIN, Evan, *Politics of Democratic Socialism.* Routledge, 1940

EDSALL, Thomas Byrne, and Mary D. EDSALL, *Chain Reaction. Race Rights and Taxes on American Politics.* Norton and Norton, 1994

FLANDERS, Alan, *The Fawley Productivity Agreement,* Faber, 1964

GOULD, Professor William B., *A Primer of American Labor Law.* MIT Press, 1982

GOULDEN, Joseph, *Meany.* Atheneum, 1972

GOULDEN, Joseph C., *Jerry Wurf, Labor's Last Angry Man.* Atheneum, 1982

HENDERSON, Sir Nicholas, *Mandarin.* Weidenfeld & Nicolson, 1994

KESSLER and BAYLISS, *Contemporary British Industrial Relations.* Macmillan, 1995

LEWIS, Congressman John, with D'ORSO, *Walking with the Wind.* Harvest Books, 1999

MEISTER and LOFTIS, *A Long Time Coming, Unionising America's Farm Workers.* Macmillan, 1977

MORRIS, Alden D., *Origins of the Civil Rights Movement.* Free Press, 1986

REUTHER, Victor G., *The Brothers Reuther.* Houghton Mifflin, 1978

ROBINSON, Derek, *Monetarism and the Labour Market.* Oxford, 1986

WEBB, Beatrice, *Our Partnership.* Longman Green, 1948

WILLS, Garry, *A Necessary Evil. American Distrust of Government.*
    Simon Schuster, 1999
WINTER, J. M., ed. *R. H. Tawney and the American Labor Movement.*
    St Martins, 1979

Commission on Industrial Relations (CIR) Reports. HMSO
    International Harvester, 1972
    Con Mech, 1973
    Associated Octel Co., 1969
Industrial Relations in the National Newspaper Industry. ACAS for the
    Royal Commission on the Press, HMSO, 1974
Worker Participation and Collective Bargaining in Western Europe.
    CIR, HMSO, 1974

ISBN 141202083-2